ISBN: 9798515687472

LEGAL DISCLAIMER:

The publisher has made every effort to ensure the accuracy of the information within this book was correct at the time of publication. Before trying a new supplement, check in with your healthcare provider. If you apply the ideas in this book, you are taking full responsibility for your actions.

www.melheatleylifecoaching.co.uk

# DEDICATION

To my beautiful mum, Ozgul Osman.

I dedicate this book to anyone suffering with their mental health, you are not alone.

To my beautiful children, Amber and Cem.
Thank you for being my biggest inspirations and supporters. I love you both very much.

To my dad, Mustafa and three big brothers,
Cengiz, Ozzie and Tarik.
Thank you all for your endless love and support.

# CONTENTS

# About the Author

Meral Osman is a survivor. She is a mum, a Certified Mindset Life Coach, Neuro-Linguistic and Mindfulness Practitioner. She is also accredited in Child Psychology and Development. Her journey to healing and self-discovery began after a traumatic incident at Tottenham Court Road station, triggering PTSD.

Her battles with anxiety started from an early age. Her mother's death at the age of just nine years old tore her entire family apart. Her father, whilst trying to keep afloat four children, sunk into his own anxiety and depression. Not long after her mother's passing, Meral was sent away to live with her overbearing grandmother in North Cyprus. She left behind her home, her three big brothers, and all that she knew in London.

Meral is now a practising Mindset Life Coach based in London, helping transform the lives of both adults and children. She currently holds motivational talks, Mindfulness workshops and is currently writing her second book.

Her journey of triumph and honesty is inspirational. If you are struggling with anxiety or simply on a journey of self-development and growth, then this book will offer you invaluable guidance and wisdom. It will teach you many techniques and exercises which you can easily implement into your day-to-day life.

# INTRODUCTION

Have you ever wanted to make a feeling stop so badly that you have contemplated doing just anything? And I mean anything. That reason alone is why I had to write this book. As someone who dreaded waking up each day, I couldn't bear the thought of battling with my debilitating physical symptoms and thoughts. Most days, I would watch the clock until 7.30pm, when I could finally put my children to bed and no longer have to deal with anyone or anything. This version of myself was only a few years ago.

I had not always felt this way. I've had waves of anxiety my entire life, but this was different, this time my body was reacting in a way that I could no longer pretend I was OK or ignore what was happening.

As we enter a recession far greater than the 1930's global economic depression. Mental health reaches breaking point for both adults and children in the UK. The devastating impact of Covid-19 not only shows through boarded-up businesses and heartache, but the stress and anxiety have overwhelmed many. Even for those who once did not think they could suffer from anxiety. The pressure pot is bubbling, and something needs to change. Perhaps you are going through a similar experience, or you may know someone that is suffering from anxiety, depression, or going through a nervous breakdown. It's time for us to all talk about the uncomfortable and spread as much love and awareness as possible.

When I was at the height of my anxiety, I thought I was going mad. Now, after many years have passed, I can call it growth. I'm now grateful for the discomfort I felt because it forced me to look within. I could no longer pretend I was OK or that the feeling would just go away. I had to face many uncomfortable truths about the people in my life, how I was choosing to live my life and most of all, I had to face my past.

Now - at 38, I am finally excited about life again and as someone who very nearly gave up, I want to tell you that you can too. You can start to live the life you truly want by taking the first small steps right now, make a choice to fight for the life you truly want. A life without limitations, without fear or a million reasons why you just can't. Make a choice right now and commit to that choice every single day.

It sounds so simple, doesn't it?

Some people might say that making a choice doesn't take the physical symptoms away. Making a choice won't stop your mind from going a hundred miles an hour and you're right it doesn't, but it's a start in the right direction. Recovery, healing, and growth are all a build-up of many small moments. Your journey will be filled with good days and challenging ones, but it's about allowing yourself to move through the storm rather than being stuck in that moment. In the beginning, your head will be full of so much noise and self-sabotage that your emotional, exhausted mind will shut you down before your rational mind has even had a chance to make a plan. Even now, you may be thinking that you just can't change, it's too late… but I promise you; you can stop this feeling that has taken over you, you can stop the endless showreel from replaying in your mind.

What I've learned during my own journey and for those that I have supported with mindset transformation is this: When you are functioning on very little energy, drowning in your own thoughts, it's almost inconceivable to believe that change is even possible. Focusing on anything other than just keeping afloat and getting through the day can be beyond overwhelming. Hence why many sufferers can never see a way out.

Stop - Breathe - Reset is a non-shouty, easily digestible yet transformational anxiety and self-help book combined. It's packed with guidance, simple exercises, thought-provoking questions, tips and, techniques that you can implement into your day-to-day life. Each exercise and question will help you open an internal dialogue that you may have avoided for quite some time.

It will offer you a new perspective, enabling you to think and feel differently. Like myself, many of my clients that have suffered from debilitating anxiety have found the techniques and exercises in this book extremely helpful and powerful. The key is repetition, patience, consistency, and most importantly self-love.

I will guide you from where you currently are in your life to where you want to be. I start at the core, the beginning that no one sees, the part that starts with you. Allowing you to embark on a truly reflective and personal journey starting with who you are and why. But… you have to believe you can change. Even if you have to fake it at first, then fake it.

Allow yourself to be honest when answering the questions. There is no right or wrong answer. It's about digging back to your inner core and re-opening the door to your soul. We are constantly growing and re-inventing ourselves. Just because you have lived a certain way for many years, or your entire life, does not mean you have to carry on living that way.

As someone who battled with anxiety, agoraphobia, OCD, imposter syndrome and PTSD…I get it. I really do. Recovery takes time, allow the waves to come, don't fight them. Stop trying to understand why you feel the way do, stop analysing every scenario, thought, and feeling. Focus on what you can do to feel better. I put so much energy and power into *why* I felt the way I did, that I rarely thought of how I wanted to feel instead.

My journey through recovery and self-discovery has been long and at the beginning, exhausting. I have tried various holistic and conventional therapies, endless medications, and quick-fix recovery programmes. They have all brought me to where I am now.

I hope this book not only offers you the reassurance and the tools you need to overcome your anxieties or unhelpful habits, but that it also helps you find the peace within to surrender your mind, heart, and soul to the possibility of living the life you truly deserve. Healing is a very personal journey. It takes patience, self-belief, and consistency, all of which are already within you.

Amongst the noise and the chaos, there is always beauty.

Pain is inevitable in life,
but suffering is optional.

*-Budda*

# TODAY I WILL BE PRESENT

*Practice the below for the next 21 days, you will see and feel the benefits. Self-awareness allows you to stop over-thinking. It reduces stress, anxiety and improves focus and concentration*

## I WILL BE PRESENT IN

- Where I am.
- What I am doing.
- Where I am going.
- Who I am with.

## I WILL BECOME AWARE OF

- My breathing.
- My posture.
- My thoughts.
- What I can smell, see, hear, feel, taste.

## TODAY I WILL

- List my daily intentions.
- Replace negative self-talk with kindness.
- Do something that makes me happy.
- I will stay committed to my daily intentions.
- Focus on my inner peace.

- Bite-size my day into digestible chunks.
- I will avoid distractions.
- Find mindful moments to just breathe.
- Practice gratitude & self-love.
- Allow myself to grow and be happy.

Through consistent repetition, you can stimulate positive thinking patterns and tap into your subconscious mind.

# FACING
# THE UNCOMFORTABLE

*Who are you, really?*

I'm going to be honest; I wasn't going to include this page. I know how irritating, annoying and uncomfortable the WHO ARE YOU question can be. Especially, when your head feels full. I've had clients walk out of sessions because this question was not the fix they were hoping for. Some call back the same day or a few days later and some never do.

When you are suffering from high levels of anxiety, your aim is to just make the feeling stop. You search externally for that 'fix', hoping something or someone can offer you a quick solution. You have very little energy to look 'within' as your subconscious feeds you with endless excuses, mine was *you cannot change, you're too tired and too far gone.* You slowly stop trusting yourself and your abilities. You forget who you are. Your very identity becomes a blur.

Sometimes we get lost between what others expect us to do and what we think we should do. The constant yo-yo-ing is exhausting both mentally and physically.

It was a grey and cold Sunday afternoon; I was visiting my dad and brothers in Stoke Newington. Hackney has changed dramatically since I was a kid growing up in the eighties. It is still predominantly filled with a large Turkish community, a million kebab shops, and endless barbers. But somehow Hackney transformed itself. It went from lock your doors and don't leave your home after 7pm to desirable and trendy. Albeit it took around 30 years for this to happen, but it happened! My Dad came over from Limassol, Cyprus in 1968, just before the war broke out. He met my beautiful mum, and they went on to have four children.

Whenever I visit Stoke Newington, I always pay a visit to the local Turkish shop that has stood strong since I was a kid. I was paying for my groceries when the new girl behind the cash register said my name. Not my abbreviated name Mel as many know me, but my full Turkish name, Meral. I was stunned, I had no idea who she was.

She went on to tell me that we were in the same art A-Level class in Enfield College, she said I was always so kind to her and that she loved my white puffa jacket. I pretended I knew her to save myself from looking foolish, but the girl she had described, studying art, always laughing, and making jokes felt like a distant stranger.

That night, when the kids were in bed, I made myself another cup of Valerian tea to calm my nerves. I started going through boxes of old photos. It held a collage of almost forgotten memories that felt so long ago. College days, travelling around Route 66 with my then best friend Leonie. Working on the Grand Prix in Abu Dhabi, the endless weekends away with friends I now barely saw. As I battled between the thoughts of *'who the hell am I?'* and *'wtf has happened to me?'* I honestly struggled to remember who I was.

I was trying so hard to fit into what was expected of me as a supportive wife, as a mother, employee, sister, daughter, as a friend. I was trying so hard to be the best at everything that I simply did not prioritise being the best version of myself. I lost focus of what made me happy in an attempt to make everyone around me happy.

Grab a pen and your notebook and get ready to get a little more uncomfortable. Sorry, but it has to be done!

Anxiety has a way of absorbing all of you, it can trick you into believing that you are weak, worthless, and not capable.

**Can you remember a time when you didn't feel anxious, how did that feel?**

**How did you carry yourself; how did you think and feel?**

**When you get up in the morning, by which standards do you live your life by?**

**Are your standards aligned with your life, is there a balance?** For example, if you're in a job that makes you miserable, but you hold great value on doing what makes you happy, then how is that aligned?

You are not just your anxious self; you are so much more. Try and remember who you are and if you can't, then start to create the person you want to become.

Remember who you are.

# PURPOSE

*A person's sense of resolve or determination.*

I often hear some of my clients tell me that they do not know what their life purpose is. Personally, I find the word purpose a little intense and misleading. We are not put on this planet to have one singular purpose. If you are searching for the one, main purpose, hoping it will find you or you will find it, then you will almost certainly be disappointed.

Purpose is allowing yourself to be truly happy and authentic in whatever setting you find yourself or in whatever profession or passion you may embark upon. Your passions are something that must make you feel internally fulfilled rather than externally. Our 'Life Purpose' is not a destiny-based phenomenon that requires deep insight. It's simply a meaningful life pursuit that we often commit to. It's allowing ourselves the freedom to try new things, explore new ideas and discover which ones ignite our soul.

Consumption is meaningless and you will forever be chasing the next possession and the next. However, if you dedicate your time to doing something that makes you come alive then this will become your focus and you will want to do it more.

Sometimes we can struggle to remember what brought us joy.

- Try reminding yourself of what you enjoyed doing as a child.
- What have you always wanted to do that you never got the chance or the time to accomplish?
- If you feel stuck, then try everything! Explore, learn, create and meet new people. Your options are limitless, you will soon find a passion that will ignite your soul.

17

# CORE IDENTITY / VALUES

*What makes you, YOU?*

Everyone holds value on different things so I'm asking you, how many of the below values mean something to you?

Grab your notebook or tick / highlight.

| | | | |
|---|---|---|---|
| Family | Beauty | Affection | Change |
| Freedom | Caring | Friendship/ | Prosperity |
| Security | Personal - | Relationship | Wellness |
| Loyalty | Development | Encouragement | Finances |
| Intelligence | Attitude | Pride in Your | Gratitude |
| Connection | Honesty | Work | Grace |
| Boundaries | Adventure | Clarity | Fun |
| Humanity | Kindness | Fun-Loving | Fame |
| Success | Teamwork | Humour | Justice |
| Diversity | Career | Leadership | Appreciation |
| Generosity | Learning | Home | Willingness |
| Integrity | Excellence | Be True | Trusting Your |
| Love | Innovation | Contentment | Gut |
| Openness | Quality | Courage | Forgiveness |
| Respect | Contributing | Balance | Self-Respect |
| Joy/Play | Spiritualism | Compassion | Abundance |
| Forgiveness | Strength | Fitness | Enjoyment |
| Excitement | Entertain | Professional | Happiness |
| Change | Wealth | Gratitude | Harmony |
| Faith | Speed | Knowledge | Peace |
| Wisdom | Power | Patience | |

18

# WHO ARE YOU?

*Grab your notebook and maybe a cup of tea.*

**Who are you and what makes you, YOU?**
Remove all the labels, your title, your gender. What are your values, capabilities, strengths, personality traits, passions, and beliefs? Write them down and be honest with yourself but if you are struggling to answer, you can always come back to this section.

**Are your core values and beliefs reflected in the below areas of your life? If so, how?**
Your Family Life/Job/Career/Relationships/Well-Being - If they are then you're probably feeling fairly content in these areas, but if they're not, then you may feel some unease. If so, start by identifying which values resonate with you and start by making them be a part of your day-to-day life.

**When do you feel most like yourself?**
When you are in environments or situations that allow you to truly be yourself, you will feel aligned with your values and identity. When you're not, you will feel a certain level of discomfort within and may find yourself pretending to be happy, just to fit in.

**In situations that feel uncomfortable - what's going on?**

- Who are you with?
- How do you feel?
- Why do you think you feel this way?

**In situations where you feel true to yourself, what's going on?**

- Who are you with?

- Is it the people or the place that makes you feel good?

**Do you ever feel...**

- Lost, confused, or stuck in your life? Y/N

- Do you have waves of imposter syndrome? Y/N

- Do you fear change and if so, why ? Y/N

If yes, then you are not alone in feeling this way. You need to work on your belief system. Raise your confidence levels by doing more of the uncomfortable.

**What you believe about yourself matters.**
You can change what you believe about yourself, but it starts with how YOU talk to yourself.  I will cover this in more depth further in the book.

*Women suffer with imposter syndrome.*

*Men suffer with imposter syndrome.*

# YOUR VALUES

*List the below eight sections in your notebook.*
*Then write down your own values for each section.*
Below are my notes.

## Health

Eat well. Drink more water. Exercise. List daily gratitude.

## Career

Find something I enjoy. Happiness. Success. Freedom. Balance. Believe in myself.

## Family Life

Spending quality time together. Less shouting. Focus on the positives. Have fun. Gratitude. Kindness. Love. Respect. Patience.

## Self- Development

Learn more. Self-belief. Self-love. Focus. Kindness. Confidence.

## Financial

Be secure. Plan for the kids and the future. Success. Be proud of myself.

## Self-Care

Kindness to myself. Routine. Structure. Priority. Self-love. Gratitude.

## Relationship(s)

Mutual respect. Love. Connection. No Judgement. Honesty. Trust. Laughter. Passion. Freedom to be me. Set boundaries. Warmth.

## Charity

Be more giving when I can. Helping others more.

Your core values are the deeply held beliefs that are in harmony with your actions and behaviour.

# THOUGHTS + FEELINGS =
## ACTIONS

*Your thoughts determine how you feel, your feelings then dictate how you act.*

You thought something awful today. It has been playing on your mind for a while. Your exhausted mind is using the little, reserve energy you have left to push the thought out, whilst another side to you pushes it straight back in. It's exhausting and overwhelming. Our thoughts have the power to debilitate us, to stop us from living out our dreams. The only way to take full control over your thoughts is by understanding that your thoughts are just ideas that you have created out of habit. The quicker you can replace them with better serving thoughts, the quicker you can start creating a healthier mindset.

**According to the National Institute of Mental Health**

Intrusive thoughts are among the symptoms of post-traumatic stress disorder (PTSD). They can also be a feature of anxiety, depression, and obsessive-compulsive disorder (OCD). They are involuntary thoughts and have no bearing on reality or a person's actual goals or desires.

Fact: People DO NOT want to act on their intrusive thoughts.

Fact: On average adults have 60,000 thoughts a day!

# Tips:

- Identify that the thoughts are intrusive.
- Remind yourself that many people have intrusive thoughts. You are not alone.
- Clarifying that they are involuntary and irrelevant to daily life.
- Do not feed the thoughts by trying to understand why you are thinking them.
- Do not believe or challenge them. Simply remind yourself that the thoughts will pass.

*"So how do we stop our mind from working against us and tune it to work for us?"*

Once you realise the true power of your own thoughts you will simply become the master of your thoughts. You are what you think yourself to be. Your mind will do and think whatever you tell it. However, if you have been playing the same internal record of self-sabotage, criticism, or fear-based scenarios then that's what you will believe. The only way to change the internal showreel is by consistent repetition.

You need to consistently make positive lifestyle changes. You need to set boundaries and start to recognise what is good and bad for you. You need to start talking to yourself in a way that is full of love and greatness.

*First step...*

Realising that you are in absolute control over your thoughts. Believing that you can change your thought process is key.

Every day, allow yourself to become aware of the thoughts you have. Don't challenge them, don't believe them. Just become aware of them and replace them with the most comforting words you would tell a friend.

# TRAIN YOUR THOUGHTS IN 14 DAYS

*You have the power to change your thinking patterns*

For the next 14 days, I would like you to write down your worries, anxieties, or just any unhelpful thoughts. Be as honest as possible, as someone who had pretty dark thoughts, I know how difficult this can be. You do not have to show this to anyone, you can pretty much burn this book or your notebook when you are done with it! But for now, we need to get what is in your head, out of it.

Next to the unhelpful thoughts write down how they make you feel and act.

Then, underneath, write down the same thought with a BUT or a WHAT IF after it. Allowing yourself to think of an alternative POSITIVE ending. Then next to it write how that positive ending makes you feel and act.

If you have been thinking a certain way for a long time, then you may feel that this will not help you (self-sabotage). However, CBT therapy and many medical professionals, scientists have proven that this method of becoming consciously AWARE of what you are thinking, writing it down and thinking of a positive alternative helps stimulate better thinking patterns. What do you have to lose? Give it a go.

You will start to see a shift in your thinking and in how you feel and act.

# 14 DAY EXERCISE

Use this page to write down any unhelpful thoughts, feelings, and actions. This allows you to become fully aware of what it is you are thinking and why you are acting in a way that is making you feel anxious / stressed.

| Thoughts | Feelings | Actions |
|---|---|---|
| *e.g. I really don't want to leave home.* | *Annoyed with myself.* | *Didn't leave the house.* |
| **But / What If** | | |
| *e.g. I really don't want to leave the house **but** I know it will be good for me .* | *Annoyed **but** I know this feeling will pass.* | *I will try my best. I took the kids out.* |
| Thoughts | Feelings | Actions |
| | | |
| | | |
| | | |
| | | |
| | | |
| | | |
| | | |

| Thoughts | Feelings | Actions |
|----------|----------|---------|
|          |          |         |
|          |          |         |
|          |          |         |
|          |          |         |
|          |          |         |
|          |          |         |
|          |          |         |
|          |          |         |
|          |          |         |
|          |          |         |
|          |          |         |
|          |          |         |
|          |          |         |
|          |          |         |

# CHASING HAPPINESS

*Sometimes happiness looks like staying at home, telling people no, and doing what makes your soul happy.*

"Are you happy?" asked the lovely Holistic, Herbalist Sarah. I had heard about her from an old friend that had seen one of my many desperate Instagram posts. I found this question a little uncomfortable, I just wanted her to pre-scribe me some pills and send me on my way. Back then, I was pretty loyal to my shitty ways so, I did what I always did - I pretended all was fine... Yes, I'm happy, I smiled. But she knew I was a broken mess, or at least my brain told me she did.

That night, my mind and body were physically reacting to my anxiety. I felt so ill, my entire body felt bruised, my legs like lead, I asked myself - Is this happiness? My autopilot, generic, I'm fine response was trying very hard to breakthrough.

For so long I had convinced myself that this was my happy, that these waves of uncertainty, stress, and panic were normal. I convinced myself that everyone feels like this at some point, life was stressful. I had accepted this version of myself without putting up a fight. But it had come to the point that my world was closing in on me and everything, even happiness, felt out of reach.

So that night, I passed on the Valerian tea and poured myself a large glass of Pinot Noir. Whilst the kids were asleep, I started dissecting each area of my life.

I had finally opened the floodgates to my mind, my suppressed emotions came pouring out and I wrote everything down. The experience was cathartic. Below is an abbreviated version of my 6-page essay.

**My two jobs:**

I hated both. Office Manager / Weekend Customer Services Assistant. This is not what I wanted.

**Marriage:**

Feel lonely and hurt. I think we're heading towards divorce.

**Kids:**

They are my world, but I'm exhausted and resent the fact I have no time for myself.

**Money:**

Where the hell does it go? I'll never get my own home.

**Health:**

I'm in constant pain with my Fibromyalgia. I've had enough of feeling like this.

**Hobbies:**

I don't have time or money for hobbies.

**Grief:**

I miss my mother, every single day.

I was so focused on my past and on all the things I did not want in my life that I had no space in my mind for what I did want. I had no idea what I wanted but I knew I did not want to live like this anymore.

My head was stuck in the past, whilst at other times I was fast-forwarding to the future. This constant yo-yo-ing was exhausting.

Pain, sadness, worry, grief, negativity followed by feeling all those emotions on a physical level. My brain was programmed into constantly playing the same showreel on repeat and I had no idea how to press stop.

**I wasn't enjoying the present moment because I wasn't in the present moment.**

Breathe...
Take a moment
to slow down.

# UNCOMFORTABLE QUESTIONS

*Grab your notebook.*

**Be truly honest with yourself, are you happy with your life?**

**What does happiness mean to you?**

Are you settling in your current life, hoping it will eventually get better and that something or someone will eventually make you happy?

Are you the - I'll be happy once I reach that destination type happiness seeker? You know the one that convinces themselves they will be happy once they get that promotion, or a bigger house, the perfect partner. Constantly basing their happiness on external factors rather than internal factors.

Perhaps you are never satisfied. An overachiever, a true perfectionist who internally criticises themselves and their achievements.

Do you find yourself playing the same showreel of self-sabotaging thoughts of it's not good enough, I can do better. Allowing no room for growth or a new perspective.

**How can you enjoy or show gratitude for what is already in front of you if your mind is already jumping onto the next big idea?**

**What would make you happy?**

**What is stopping you from living this life?**

Looking within is hard. It's a long and exhausting journey that involves facing the horrible parts of us we have avoided for a long time. But the benefits are life-changing, the power you gain from living the life you truly want is happiness. It's the freedom to like all of you and to live a life that makes your soul come alive. Why settle for anything less when you deserve all the happiness in the world.

You may have to make sacrifices.

You may have to let people down.

You may have to become uncomfortable for a while, but the result of living a truly authentic life will be worth it.

# STAY FOCUSED ON YOU

*Grab your notebook and answer the below as honestly as possible*

To stimulate better-thinking patterns, we must first start to shift our focus onto other areas of our lives. It's important to view your life from all angles and to build an internal positive self-talk system.

**WHY?** So, you can train your internal dialogue to be the best it can be, to increase the positivity volume so it can become louder and stronger. This will help build on your confidence, self-esteem, and internal dialogue.

**20** **things that make you internally happy.**
Think about what makes you feel content.

**15** **things you are most grateful for.**
Shifting your focus onto what you are grateful for allows you to remove your focus from all that feels wrong in your life. Being grateful opens your vibration to receiving more goodness and less negativity.

**10** **things that you are most proud of.**
Remind yourself of all your capabilities, strengths, and achievements. Think of what you want to add to the list as time goes on and keep adding to it.

**5** **wishes you would make if you knew they would come true and why?**

Really think about this, do not limit yourself here. What would you really wish for and why?

**2** **things you would like to do /achieve before you die.**

Think BIG, do not limit yourself to what you think you can do. Think about what it is you want to do.

# STOP – BREATHE – CHECK-IN

*A page to come to when you feel…*

You're going to be ok. Remember, this feeling will pass. You have felt this way before and you have been fine. Allow yourself to acknowledge and feel your emotions, don't fight them. Respond to the feelings you are experiencing with kindness, compassion, and love, as if you knew they were coming. Fighting how you feel or trying to stop it will only escalate your panic and heart rate.

If you feel disorientated or overwhelmed, have a focus reference point. Focus your vision on one thing/object, whilst you create a moment of calm within.

Take a moment to pause, close your eyes and breathe deep and slow. Allow your mind to think of your happy place.

Inhale 1,2,3,4 from your nose

Exhale 1,2,3,4 from your mouth.

**Focus your attention on what you can;**
*Smell, hear, taste, see, feel.*

This allows you to bring yourself back to the present moment.

# STOP – BREATHE – AFFIRMATIONS

*Affirmations can help our brains develop new,
positive shortcuts.*

It is well established that in the brain the neurons that fire together, wire together. When we think about something repeatedly, the neurons get wired together strongly. It takes repetition and consistency.

## Repeat

I am safe, I am safe, I am safe.

I know this feeling will pass. I am in full control of my thoughts. Like a warm gentle wave passing over my body. This moment will pass.

With every breath I take; I inhale peace, calmness and exhale my fears and worries.

I am focused on my journey of self-development and recovery.

I know this feeling cannot hurt me.

My thoughts cannot hurt me, I am in control of my thoughts.

We are only limited
by the ideas we create
in our mind.

# UNDERSTANDING ANXIETY

*Anxiety is an emotion characterised by a feeling of intense worry.*

Everyone feels anxiety to some degree, for example, you can be anxious about an upcoming job interview. You have butterflies in your stomach and might even have a nervous poo just before. However, someone who suffers from high levels of anxiety fixates on what could go wrong. They will over analyse the journey there, have endless safety behaviours in place to make sure they are doing all they can to get through the day. They will experience debilitating physical symptoms daily. Now, throw in agoraphobia, and slowly the person starts to feel like they are shrinking. Everything around them gets bigger, louder, scarier, and faster.

I remember feeling like I was LIVING AMONGST FIERCE GIANTS. The noises, the lights, the sensations. I constantly felt like I was on a wobble board, navigating through their booming voices whilst trying to avoid being crushed by their weight.

Anxiety is the brains' way of alerting us of danger, when the brain thinks you are in danger it triggers the release of hormones which include ADRENALINE and CORTISOL. When the situation is over, the hormones are supposed to go back to their normal levels. However, if you have suffered from long periods of stress, forever burning yourself out, then voilà - you kick-start your AUTOMATIC FEAR RESPONSE.

Anxiety can be a great motivator; we need it to survive, and we need it to protect us to a certain degree. If we are in danger, anxiety pops up, alerting us. But what happens when it does not want to leave?

## WHERE THE HELL IS THE OFF BUTTON?

# HIGH FUNCTIONING ANXIETY

*People with high-functioning anxiety, while proud of their achieve-*
*ments, are often plagued by thoughts of disappointing others,*
*criticism, and rejection.*

Learning to be present did not come naturally to me. I was a high-function-ing anxiety addict and we worked well together for a long time. I would complete tasks at record speed and if I'm totally honest, I enjoyed over-doing and over-pleasing. It gave me a sense of worth. Now looking back, I can see that I rarely considered what I wanted or what I needed. I was enjoying the buzz of showing those around me that I could handle anything. I could work two unfulfilling jobs, I could raise two kids and not ask for help, I could be in severe pain with my fibromyalgia and not moan to anyone. This refusal to seek help was all down to my unhelpful mindset, I refused to look weak.

I would stretch myself so thin that I was actually known for it. I was known as the good girl who never said no in fear of confrontation or upsetting others, I was a total people pleaser. How sad is that? Where were my boundaries? I got a huge buzz (external validation) from showing everyone how capable and strong I was. I wore my stress like a badge of honour!

## 'So, are you telling me there is nothing wrong with me, yet my body is telling me there is?"

When my doctor told me there was nothing wrong with me, I thought of two things. Either she's mad, or I am. Every single fibre in my body was palpitating. This can't be normal I thought. I mean, I switched my morning Latte to three cups of valerian tea, something was wrong!

I convinced myself that the doctors had missed something. I had MRI scans, endless blood tests, ECG scans, the long list could go on. I refused to accept responsibility for the mess I had created. My identity was formed around my negative and unhealthy beliefs about myself. I had this embedded seed from my childhood that the more I multi-tasked the better person I was. I wish I could go back and give that girl a hug.

Does any of this sound familiar? If you feel like your life is going a 100mph in a direction that feels uncomfortable then you need to start asking your-self some uncomfortable questions and don't be afraid to hear the answers. Learn to be fully present in what you are doing. If you are not happy in a certain area(s) of your life, work on them if you can. If not, accept it and move forward. Show gratitude for all that you have without worrying about the 'what ifs' life could throw at you.

YOUR LIFE will become whatever you want or create it to be, so if you are creating chaos in your mind, you will only receive more chaos. Create a world based on what matters to you, your beliefs, and values. Not what others expect from you. Do not fall for the comparison trap, there will always be someone with less or more than you. Be grateful for your current life but still commit to growth.

## UK Population
### Mid-year estimate (2020)
## 67,081,000
### 20 March and 30 March 2020
### almost half
## (49.6%)
### of people in Great Britain
### reported "high" (rating 6 to 10) anxiety.

How does your anxiety stop you living your best life? What would you do differently if you did not feel this way?

# ANXIETY SYMPTOMS

*Be honest, how often do you Google your symptoms?*

Once, five, or maybe even two thousand times a day? Starting from today, **PLEASE STOP!** You are only fuelling your anxiety even more. If you are unsure of your symptoms, then please speak to a medical professional and if your anxiety is making you believe that every medical professional is wrong (as mine did) then please learn to reassure yourself.

## Anxiety has endless symptoms, here are just a few;

- Feel like you are drowning.
- Legs feel like jelly.
- Slurred speech.
- Pins and needle sensations.
- Fearful / Scared.
- Fuzzy head.
- Heavy legs, almost like lead.
- Pain in the eyes.
- Intrusive thoughts.
- Constantly on high alert.
- Feeling wired.
- Dizzy.
- Tearful.
- Overwhelmed.
- Mild Hallucinations.
- Irritable.
- Paranoid.
- Unhappy.
- Constantly exhausted.
- Panic attacks.
- Tight chest.
- Sensitive tummy.
- Nerve endings feel alive.
- Claustrophobic.
- Palpitations.
- Backache.
- Nauseous.
- Senses heightened.
- Grinding teeth.
- Disassociation.
- Breathlessness

**How many of these symptoms do you have?**

Perhaps you have more or less... If you suffer from any of these physical symptoms, you should be extremely proud of yourself for getting through the day. You are simply amazing, always remember that. But please remember that you do not have to keep suffering. Keep reading this book to discover the long list of holistic remedies that have proven to be extremely beneficial.

**How do you feel when you look at the symptoms?**

Do the words make you feel anything? Look at breathlessness, dizzy, tight chest... words are immensely powerful. If you think of a word for long enough, you will also feel the association that comes with it. This is why it is vital to soothe your anxiety instead of intensifying the feeling by thinking/ visualising the worst-case scenario.

**"How do I implement change when I am constantly battling with heart palpitations, dizzy spells, etc?"**

Implementing change is hard in the beginning. But at some point, you have to make a choice. Because the alternative, of staying like this is not living. It's simply existing and you were put on this earth to do far more than just exist.

Take baby steps and just start letting go of the things that don't really matter. Once you start, you will build up daily momentum. 10 minutes a day, will turn into 20 minutes, 30 minutes, maybe even an hour a day of making a few simple lifestyle changes. Accept that recovery takes time. You have to help yourself; you have to want more for your life and be willing to implement a healthier mindset, one that makes you feel excited about life again.

Recovery is a process of learning how to change your relationship with anxiety, fear and most importantly changing your self-belief system... It's learning to ask yourself uncomfortable questions and facing your truths without panicking.

If your physical symptoms are debilitating your day-to-day life, then please do speak to a medical professional. It took me nearly three years of daily suffering to finally speak to my GP about these issues. After consulting with them I realised the right path for me was medication. However, medication may not be the right choice for you, but it is one that you should investigate. There are so many different types of medication so you should do your own research and if you have any concerns or worries then speak to your GP about them. You do not have to suffer.

# YOUR BRAIN AND ANXIETY

## THE AMYGDALA

Fear is produced when your amygdala, a primitive part of the brain's limbic system involved in the processing and expression of emotion, kicks in to ensure survival. Your amygdala's job is to detect if there is any threat in the environment. If it does, it sends a signal down near our kidneys, releasing adrenaline. It withdraws blood from our hands/stomach, and it pumps more blood to our heads. Sending signals to fight, flight, and freeze.

Anxiety can make your brain hyperactive to threats. When you deal with anxiety consistently, your amygdala grows larger. The amygdala is a tiny almond-shaped structure located in the limbic system.

## PRE-FRONTAL CORTEX

This brain region has been implicated in planning complex cognitive behaviour, personality expression, decision making, and moderating social behaviour. Research suggests that most human brains take about 25 years to develop, though these rates can vary among men and women. Although the human brain matures in size during adolescence, important developments within the prefrontal cortex and other regions still take place well into one's 20s.

Anxiety weakens the connections between the amygdala and the prefrontal cortex. When the amygdala alerts the brain of danger, the prefrontal cortex should kick in and help you come up with a rational, logical response. In non-anxious brains, the prefrontal cortex responds rationally when the amygdala sends out alerts. This process doesn't work the same in anxious brains. Instead, when the amygdala alerts the PFC to danger, the connection is weak. Thus, the rational, problem-solving part of the brain isn't heard, which can lead to irrational thoughts and erratic behaviour.

## THE VAGUS NERVE

The vagus nerve (also known as the 10th cranial nerve or CN X) is a very long nerve that originates in the brain stem and extends down through the neck and into the chest and abdomen. It carries both motor and sensory information, and it supplies innervation to the heart, major blood vessels, airways, lungs, oesophagus, stomach, and intestines.

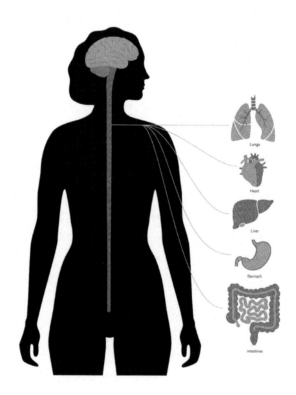

# Tips:

In order to tone up your vagal nerve and relax your nervous system, here are some very powerful and effective things you can do:

- Deep and slow diaphragmatic breathing into your belly (especially longer exhalations, such as using the 4-7-8 technique.
- Singing, chanting, and gargling.
- Humming Meditation.
- Cold exposure (e.g., taking a cold shower, splashing cold water on your face and sauna).
- Meditation.
- Exercise (especially weightlifting, HIIT, cardio and daily walking for 30-60 minutes) Massage (especially foot massage).
- Body scan and Yoga Nidra.
- Massaging your diaphragm.
- Foam rolling and Yin Yoga (to work with tension in the fascia).
- Transformational Breathwork.
- Sound Healing.

# THE THREE MINDS

When you align your head, your heart, and your gut, you avoid internal conflicts which in psychology is called "cognitive dissonance". It's a balance you need to find every time you face a decision. To successfully listen to the head, the heart, and the gut, it requires focus and awareness from you. It comes with dedication and practice.

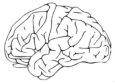

### HEAD
**You know**

Logic, reason, answers
& knowledge.
Useful if clear and focused.

### HEART
**You feel**

Feeling, love, authentic, emotional.
Useful for offering a deeper
connection at expressing yourself.

### GUT
**Instinct**

Instinctive, nervous response and
past experiences.
Useful for when making quick
decisions.

# I JUST CAN'T DO IT!

My legs felt like lead, my head was spinning. The sound of the sea of people outside Liverpool Street Station felt like a stampede of wild animals crushing every inch of my body.

I just wanted to get home to my babies.

I called my brother who worked nearby. I felt like my body was sinking into the ground. I couldn't physically get myself on the train home. I could barely speak to him as I just closed my eyes to avoid the sensory overload. I was terrified. That night, my big brother took me home.

Every thought possible bombarded my mind. *You're useless, what kind of person can't even get themselves home. You're so weak. What if it happens again?*

# AGORAPHOBIA

*When you fear open, crowded spaces and being away from a place of safety.*

In 2017, I was pushed down the escalators at Tottenham Court Road Station.

In the 5-10 seconds that my body tumbled down the escalators, I had a few thoughts;

**"I am never going to see my babies again."**
**"Am I going to die today?"**
**"Is this a terrorist attack?"**

Luckily, it wasn't a terrorist attack. Just a seven-foot, rugby player-sized drunken man falling upon all eight stone and 5'3" of me. Surprisingly, I was fine, I had no visible marks and I just carried on with my journey home. What I noticed weeks after the incident was something in me had changed, I became hypervigilant. I mean I was always on high alert, but this was all consuming.

A few weeks later, I remember having to go into work earlier than usual to assist the company's Chief Director that had flown over from the United States. I woke up late and pretty much threw myself out of the house without my usual coffee fix and a slice of toast.

I remember feeling miserable and exhausted as I squeezed myself onto a busy Central Line filled with Christmas shoppers and tourists.

I never liked the tube, but that day something in me didn't feel right. My ears echoed the noises around me, I felt an overwhelming sense of heat rush around my body. I was still seven stops away from work as more bodies pressed up against me. My legs felt paralyzed.

I didn't want to be there, I just wanted to go home.

Alarm bells rung when my heart started pounding through my chest. "Am I having a heart attack?" I looked around hoping no one would notice, I felt powerless. My throat tightened as the flood gates to my mind had fully opened, endless thoughts drowned every ounce of my rationality. Moments after this my body had completely shut down.

Yep, I was that annoying person fainting on the Central Line probably causing major delays.

A person who suffers from agoraphobia finds it extremely difficult to leave their safe place. Making endless excuses on why they have had to cancel commitments, why they are once again late for work. Constantly fearful that others will think they are mad, or that no one will understand. The biggest issue I had was, I thought I was going mad and if I thought I was going mad, then surely others did too.

As the weeks and months went on something in me changed.

| | | |
|---|---|---|
| Getting in the car | = | I will crash and die. |
| Getting the tube | = | I feel trapped, claustrophobic. |
| Being away from home | = | I do not feel safe. |
| Taking my children out | = | What if I have a panic attack and faint? |
| Visiting somewhere new | = | What if I can't find the exit. |

## Is agoraphobia common?

1-3%

of the population suffer with agoraphobia.
It is twice as common in women as it is in men.

# MANAGING YOUR ANXIETY

*Proven tips that can help bring clarity and inner peace*
*to your day-to-day life.*

## SPEAK TO A MEDICAL PROFESSIONAL

If you have not already then please do speak to your GP, you do not have to suffer. There is support and guidance that can help alleviate your physical and emotional symptoms.

## PRACTICE SELF-AWARENESS / MINDFULNESS

Self-awareness is the conscious knowledge of one's own character, feelings, motives, and desires. Make a conscious effort to be aware of your thoughts, behaviour, and actions. When we start to become aware of any unhelpful thoughts, we can then take the power away from them by changing our internal response.

## AVOID UNHEALTHY DISTRACTIONS

Learning to avoid distractions in a world full of distractions isn't easy. Especially when the biggest distraction of all (our phones) can also be used to escape our very own reality.

In order to overcome distractions, you need to understand what drives your behaviours. **What prompts you to compulsively look at your phone or read one more email?**

The root cause of human behaviour is the desire to escape discomfort. Even when we think we are seeking pleasure, we're actually driven by the desire to free ourselves from the pain of wanting. The truth is, we overuse video games, social media, and our mobile phones not just for the pleasure they provide, but because they free us from psychological discomfort.

Distraction, then, is an unhealthy escape from bad feelings. Once you can recognise the role internal triggers like boredom, loneliness, insecurity, fatigue, and uncertainty play in your life, you can decide how to respond in a healthier manner. You can't control how you feel, but you can learn to control how you react to the way you feel.

- Turn off unnecessary notifications.
- Avoid endlessly scrolling through your social media feeds.
- No phones/screen-time when having dinner.
- Have a set time of the day that you will check your work emails.
- Allow yourself to be bored or uncomfortable.

## FIND YOUR WHY

Why do you NOT want to feel this way? Why are you dedicated to your journey of inner peace and growth? Use that as your focus and motivation. **Write it down and read it daily.**

## LISTEN TO YOUR BODY

What do you need right now? Acknowledge, soothe, and reassure your anxiety.

## LOVE YOURSELF

Make a commitment to yourself to never give up. Some days will be uncomfortable and other days will be great. Focus on the great ones and make more of them.

Learn to praise yourself. Positive internal dialogue is so important. Do not beat yourself up for feeling the way you do. That's not going to help you. Move forward and keep focused on your journey ahead.

## BREATHE THROUGH THE CHOAS

Try not to over-analyse why you feel the way you do. This is not going to help you. Don't challenge your anxiety or thoughts, focus on how you want

*Reference: Psychology Today*

to feel rather than why you feel this way. When your head feels full, remove yourself away from where you are, close your eyes and take slow and deep breathes. This will help calm your nervous system down.

## CREATE CALM MOMENTS

Deep relaxation offers you a moment to just stop – breathe and reset. Meditation is not for everyone; it took me years to truly become comfortable with it as I always thought I was doing it wrong. The more I tried to control my thoughts the more my mind went into overdrive. After practising for many years, I now see there is no right or wrong way. It's simply giving yourself the time to focus on your breathing and to feel what is already within you.

## EXPAND YOUR COMFORT ZONE

Day by day, do a little more of what makes you feel uncomfortable. If you know it will lead to growth and help you on your life journey, then do it. Small steps will lead to big steps. But you need to start and keep the momentum going. Allow the setbacks to happen, there is a lesson to learn even in the days that are not so great. Look for the good and don't focus on the bad.

## ROUTINE

Implement a healthy daily routine and better serving mindset

- Eat well and drink plenty of water.

- Take your vitamins / supplements.

- Surround yourself with positive people that inspire you.

- Get at least 8-9 hours' sleep a day.

- Be disciplined with your routine and be organised.

## SAFETY BEHAVIOURS

Have healthy distractions or safety behaviours if this makes you feel more secure at first. As you gain more confidence in your abilities, remind yourself that these are only temporary solutions.

e.g. I would not leave the house without a bottle of water in case I felt faint. I would take a puzzle to the park for me and my children just so I had something to do if I felt dizzy.

## AVOID ALCOHOL / SMOKING / DRUGS

- This will only increase your anxiety.

# 5
# GROUNDING TECHNIQUES

*bring yourself back to the present moment*

Cover Your Crown.

**Feel Your Feet.**

Follow Your Breath.

**Stand Like a Tree.**

Take a Cold Shower.

## "How do I implement change when I feel mentally exhausted, drained, and I have nothing left in me?"

Start by making small lifestyle changes. Recovery takes time and is very personal to each person. There is no right or wrong way to recover. Start implementing a healthy daily routine and a better serving mindset. Perhaps you need to accept some stuff or let go of years' worth of mental torture or memories.

If you are miserable about your current life then honestly ask yourself, what could you do that is manageable and doable to accept and move forward?

Try not to overwhelm yourself with endless tasks. Do what you can manage, write down a few things you would like to do that day and do not criticise yourself if you do not carry them out. Listen to your body. I remember a time when simply getting out of bed, feeding my children, and emptying the dishwasher was good enough. We were alive and safe.

Work on building up your confidence, your strengths and awareness of your abilities. What do you love doing? Do more of it. Don't worry about making others uncomfortable or what others will think. Making yourself comfortable and happy is the priority, nothing else matters.

I'm not telling you to become a selfish arsehole. But if you are forever squeezing into everyone else's expectations of you then you will never be internally satisfied.

I always tell my clients to look at how they internally talk to themselves, if you say things like: I'm tired all the time, I'm constantly in pain, I hate my life, I hate my body, I'm too fat / too skinny. I feel out of control, I don't know what I want from life - then how do you think you will feel?

If you are constantly focusing on how you don't want to feel rather than how you do want to feel, you will only feel the same.

# FOCUS ON HOW YOU WANT TO FEEL

Make a conscious effort to focus less on the stress in your life and more on what you actually want for your life. You will soon see a shift in your thinking and in the way you feel. Thinking positively did not come naturally to me. I was a born pessimist that was constantly self-criticising and doubting others.

How you do you want to feel? Calm, relaxed, happy, fulfilled... whatever you want to feel, think about what YOU NEED TO DO to feel those things.

Maybe it's a case of 'doing less' of what you don't enjoy and 'more' of what you do enjoy?

Life isn't meant to be easy.
It's about creating moments
that fill your heart with
warmth and joy.
It's about finding happiness
in the everyday, boring stuff.
It's about appreciating all that
you have whilst striving for
what you want.

# DRIVING WITH ANXIETY

*Trust yourself and your abilities.*

Do you remember why you first wanted to drive? Do you remember the feeling you had when you heard those three words, 'you have passed'! I remember questioning my examiner – "are you sure, I've actually passed?" I was so in denial of my own abilities. Why did I not celebrate my wins instead of questioning them? I had zero confidence in my abilities. If you are struggling to drive at the moment because of your racing thoughts, then please know you are not alone.

## Tips:

### GET MORE LESSONS

Getting more lessons with an experienced instructor will help you practice driving with someone who you know can take full control at any time. Practice on the roads you have been avoiding and explain that you feel anxious. Being honest about how you feel will make you feel less anxious.

### SIT IN THE CAR

If you cannot bring yourself to drive, try sitting in the car for 10 minutes without driving. Listen to the radio, read a book. Just start feeling more comfortable in your car.

### SHOW GRATITUDE

Show the car some love, treat it to a car wash, remind yourself of how lucky you are to be able to have a car, especially on rainy days. Showing gratitude does not mean you shouldn't feel what you feel. It is just a great way to remind yourself of the positives about driving.

## BE PREPARED

Make sure your phone is charged and you have a reliable sat nav.
Keep a spare phone charger in your car.
Always make sure you have enough petrol before setting out

## PLAN YOUR ROUTE

Rather than avoid driving, plan your route. Really break it down. Have a half-way mark, give yourself a five-minute rest stop (even if you are only driving for 20mins) it's just a great way to bite-size the drive rather than seeing it as an overwhelming task.

## TAKE AN EXPERIENCED DRIVER WITH YOU

Take an experienced driver with you but do not rely on this method all the time. See it as a temporary means to get you going. If it helps you for now, then that's great but keep pushing yourself when you are ready for the next step.

## GET SOME AIR

Open your window and feel the breeze come in.

## LEARN TO TRUST AND REASSURE YOURSELF

When a thought comes into your mind reassure yourself - I am safe, I am capable, I am in control, and I am confident in my abilities.

## CELEBRATE YOUR WINS

Self-praise is massively important, even if you just got in the car and started the engine after not being able to do it for so long. Be proud of yourself. Every day, try a little more and gradually you will feel so much better.

# STOP – BREATHE – DRIVE

*Find 5-10 minutes to quieten your mind and reassure yourself before driving.*

## Repeat the below affirmations.

I accept I may feel anxious, but I will soothe, calm, and reassure my anxiety, not fear it.

I am capable.

I am confident.

I trust myself.

I am safe.

I want more for my life.

I am in the process of learning to push myself.

This is NOT the life I accept for myself.

I am in control of my thoughts.

I am in control of my life.

I am safe, I am safe, I am safe.

You are in control of your
thoughts, feelings, behaviour,
actions & future.

# IMAGINE

How different your life could be in 6 months' time.
Keep pushing and believing in yourself.

Change is good.

Never be afraid to do the uncomfortable, nothing is out of your reach, it's just your unhelpful thoughts that make you feel that they are. Always celebrate how far you have come.

**You are amazing, keep going.**

# PARENTHOOD & ANXIETY

*You are not alone*

I'm not sure if writing this at 8.45pm after battling for over an hour to get my two kids to sleep is a great idea but here it goes. I'll try and keep it somewhat optimistic to those that might be expecting their first bundle of joy or planning to have children in the future.

I was twenty-nine when I had my beautiful baby girl Amber. I was somewhat anxiety-free and full of pure excitement. I just remember wanting to give this tiny little person the best possible start in life, I felt so many emotions. However, no one warns you about the relentlessness of the first year, my daughter had severe acid reflux and just refused to sleep. For the first six months, I cried a lot and then felt extremely guilty for feeling all those things. So, I did what I always did back then, refused help, pretended that all was fine and carried on silently crying on my bathroom floor.

Parenthood naturally opens thoughts we never had to think about before. Some healthy, exciting thoughts but for me, they were mostly quite morbid ones. My long list of intrusive thoughts all boiled down to my fear of dying and leaving my two kids behind, just like my mother had left me.

My anxiety didn't fully manifest until I had my second child, by this point my marriage which had a good spell was spiralling downhill and every single alarm bell in my body was ringing. Suddenly I went from having my perfect little family to facing the prospect of raising two little kids on my own. I was petrified.

During the first years of motherhood, I was in the mummy bubble. I completely threw my identity out of the window and made no time to prioritise my needs.

Now, as a newly divorced, single mum, I still have anxious moments. I think about the impact divorce has had on my children. I have moments when I lose my patience and wish I hadn't. I question myself, doubt myself and beat myself up but I'm finally OK with all of that. These moments are no longer daily, they no longer consume my every thought or make me feel like shit. I've learnt to remind myself that I'm doing my best and I have overcome things I never thought I could, I hope you know that you can too.

## Tips:

### PLEASE ASK FOR HELP

Do not burn yourself out in an attempt to show the world how capable you are. Pushing your body and mind to extreme exhaustion will only lead to you physically reacting to your burnout.

### YOU WON'T HAVE ALL THE ANSWERS

I remember talking to my daughter about something that was really bothering her. The more I tried to calm her down the more I seemed to make matters worse. I asked her why this situation bothered her so much, it wasn't a big deal. She looked me straight in the eyes, tears aside and said it's a big deal to me, it means something to me. I had forgotten that at the age of (I think she was 7) that there was no room for rationality, I just had to be present, give her a cuddle and let her have her moment.

### ENJOY THE LITTLE MOMENTS

The Friday night movie nights or winter walks in the forest, whatever your family love doing, make the time to do it.

### DON'T OVER PLAN

If you've just had a baby then enjoy the baby bubble, give yourself and your baby time to adjust to all the changes. The first year is a beautiful time but also a very challenging one.

## MUM/DAD GUILT

Is in all of us.... When I lost my job, I had pangs of guilt for not being able to give my children the after-school activities they wanted to do or the freedom to just go out when we wanted. Then, I secured a job and had even more guilt as I barely saw them. Even as I type this, my children are no doubt on their iPads, filling their bellies with sugar filled treats. Parenthood is challenging. Whether you're doing it alone or with your partner, it's a constant juggle. We have to find the balance, guilt should not be there to make us feel bad, or to make us overcompensate when we are with our children. Guilt should be a great reminder of the sacrifices we sometimes have to make for our health, peace of mind or their future.

## EMBRACE THE MADNESS

Some days will be a breeze, you'll sleep, your baby will sleep, and everything will just fall into place. Some days will be utter chaos, embrace those days and find the beauty in the madness of it all.

## DON'T FALL FOR THE COMPARISON TRAP

Just because your new NCT friend (parent group) is speaking three languages to her new-born and only feeds them homegrown produce whilst running her weekly timetable down your throat, DOES NOT MEAN THAT'S HOW YOU SHOULD DO THINGS. Your family, your way. Same principle if your children are older, everyone's circumstances and choices are different, do what feels right for your family.

## TALK

If something doesn't feel right, talk to a medical professional, or a close family member or friends, you'll be surprised how many people have felt the same. You are not weak or less able for being honest about how you feel. You are showing great strength by doing what will ultimately help you and your family. I struggled talking to my GP, I just hated the thought of being judged or coming across as mad. What if my children are talking away from? Be the truth is those were just my thoughts, the only person judging me was, me.

## LETTING GO

Don't try and control every little thing. You will forever be disappointed, angry, and irritated when things do not go your way. Learn to let go and see things from other people's perspectives, especially if you know your perfectionism is disruptive to the people around you.

## LOOKING AFTER YOU

Self-care is not something that came naturally to me. It felt way too over-indulgent and selfish to make time for me. How could I justify spending an hour at the gym or having a coffee on my own when the laundry was piling up and the dishwasher needed to be unloaded or loaded for the millionth time. The truth is those jobs NEVER END. Some days, you just have to put something amazing on, do your hair a little different, wear the shoes you've been saving for a special occasion and just get the hell out of the house.

## LEARN TO SAY NO

Start today. One of the best things I ever did was learning to not take on the things I never really wanted to.

Early parenthood isn't always a magical, bonding time.
It's full of self-doubt, relentless night feeds, exhaustion, and everything in between.
Each stage of parenthood has its challenges and triumphs. It's OK not to enjoy every moment.

# ANGER

*A strong feeling of annoyance, displeasure, or hostility.*

We all get angry at times, but if you find yourself losing your cool over every little thing, if it's disrupting your work or home life then you need to look at where that anger is coming from. Usually, when a person experiences anger, it may relate to them feeling overwhelmed, powerless, scared, or threatened.

QUESTIONS *Grab your notebook and answer the following.*

- When are you most angry?
- Where does your anger come from, are you aware?
- How do you feel after getting angry? Remorseful, annoyed, sad, frustrated?
- How would you like to feel instead?
- What could you do to help yourself calm down?

## HOW TO MANAGE YOUR ANGER

- Close Eyes/Slow Breathing.
- Don't blame others for your outbursts, take responsibility and move on.
- Learn to step back.
- Practice Mindfulness. This will allow you to stay present in the moment and be aware of your emotions and thoughts.
- Make a list of what triggers you.
- Make a 4-week diary, listing, when and where you felt angry.
- Manage your expectations about what it is that is making you angry.
- Ask yourself, will this really matter in a years' time?
- Make a conscious effort and choice to be less reactive.
- Write down how you would like to behave instead.
- When you feel yourself becoming angry, count to 15 in your mind.

# MEDICATION

*"It took me nearly three years of absolute mental and physical torture to finally accept medication".*

I believed that accepting medication meant I had failed to make myself better. I desperately wanted to not mask my symptoms or become addicted to antidepressants. But the truth is, if I hadn't taken medication, I would not have been able to study. I certainly wouldn't have been able to write this book or do all the things that I do with my children.

Medication for me was the start, it helped with the physical sensations, but I also had to work hard on changing my mindset. I had to change many lifestyles factors, medication is not the cure, it's a chance to get off the wobble board, remove the fog, and start thinking clearly.

If you are thinking about exploring the medication route but you're afraid of becoming addicted or reliant then please know that suffering from your daily symptoms is far worse.

Speak to your GP, there are many types of medications suited to your experiences and how you are feeling.

# ALLOW THE UNCOMFORTABLE DAYS

*"Your body will do whatever your mind is telling it, start seeing the beauty in each day. Even the challenging ones, for there is always something to learn or to be grateful for from a not-so-great day".*

Stop fighting the not-so-great days. Perhaps this is just your intuition's way of telling you to stop and listen. What is going on when you feel this way? Are your thoughts making you believe all is bad or has something happened?

The difference between me now and me three years ago, is that I no longer call my uncomfortable days, bad days. I have finally allowed myself to acknowledge and self-soothe rather than panic and tense up.

Not fighting your thoughts puts you in full control, it means you have uncomfortable days rather than dragging out that feeling for weeks or even months.

## Tips:

- Listen to your body & intuition. What are you craving?
- Meditation will help clear your mind and relax your body.
- Drink plenty of water.
- Eat healthily. Cut out all sugary / processed foods.
- Cancel commitments if you have to.
- Set healthy boundaries.
- Prioritise your mental health.
- Switch off your phone or turn off notifications.
- Get some fresh air.
- Rest.

# PLEASE DON'T...

Over analyse why you feel the way you do. Just put your focus on soothing yourself. Don't beat yourself up. Everyone has challenging days.

## Think about, what is your body craving right now?

- Freedom
- Rest
- Commitment
- Security
- Confidence
- Comfort

- Time
- Balance
- Self-Esteem
- Support
- Energy
- Reassurance

Listen to your needs and make space in your life to implement what your soul, mind and body are craving. Take the time to clear and soothe your mind.

Learn to trust your intuition.
What is the discomfort you are
feeling? What do you need?

# FEARS / PHOBIAS

*Is an emotion / irrational fear that is focused
on a particular entity.*

Fear arises with the threat of harm, either physical, emotional, or psychological, real or **imagined.** Fear serves an important role in keeping us safe as it protects us when we are in danger.

However, if you suffer from high levels of anxiety and have kicked off your automatic fear response, then you may feel like you are constantly in danger. A number of regions in the brain are involved in sensing and responding to stimuli that result in the fear response. A person with a phobia either tries to avoid the thing that triggers the fear or endures it with great anxiety and distress.

**Phobias are the most common type of anxiety disorder.
In the UK, an estimated**

# 10 million people
**have phobias.
Phobias can affect anyone,
regardless of age, sex, and social background.**

**Phobias can be divided into two main categories.**

- Simple Phobias
- Complex Phobias

*Reference: NHS*

## SIMPLE PHOBIAS:

Simple phobias are fears about specific objects, animals, situations or activities. Some common examples include:

- **dogs**
- **spiders**
- **snakes**
- **enclosed spaces**
- **dentists**
- **flying**

Phobias affect different people in different ways. Some people only react with mild anxiety when confronted with the object of their fear, while others experience severe anxiety or have a severe panic attack.

## COMPLEX PHOBIAS:

Complex phobias tend to be more disabling than simple phobias because they are often associated with a deep-rooted fear or anxiety about a particular circumstance or situation. Two common examples of complex phobias are agoraphobia and social phobia.

## AGORAPHOBIA

Is a fear of being in situations where escape might be difficult, or help wouldn't be available if things go wrong.

A person with agoraphobia may be scared of:

- travelling on public transport
- visiting a shopping centre
- and in the most severe cases – leaving home

## SOCIAL PHOBIA

Is a fear of social situations, such as weddings, or performing in social situations, such as public speaking. People with a social phobia have a fear of embarrassing themselves or of being humiliated in public.

# MOST COMMON FEARS

Fear of failure.

Fear of not being successful.

Fear of becoming ill.

Fear of missing out. FOMO.

Fear of dying (thanatophobia¬)

Fear of losing a loved one.

Fear of rejection.

Fear of judgement.

Fear of uncertainty.

Fear of loneliness.

Fear of debt.

Fear of disappointment.

# 0-5
# THINKING

## Someone without anxiety

| 0 | 2 | 3 | 4 | 5 |
|---|---|---|---|---|
| No anxiety | Worrying thought | Process with facts + reassurance | Acknowledge | Carry on with their day |

## Someone with anxiety

| 0 | 2 | 3 | 4 | 5 |
|---|---|---|---|---|
| No anxiety | Worrying thought | Process by adding FEAR + PANIC | Validates fears as if real | In state of panic or fear. |

## "Sound familiar"?

# The Hierarchy of Fear

0 - Calm.

1 - Apprehension (because your environment does not feel safe).

2 - Concern – You are or think you are in danger.

3 - Fight, Flight or Freeze.

4 - Helplessness – begin to panic & lose touch with reality.

5 - Loss of sense.

6 - Death (you think you are dying).

# Hierarchy of Staying Calm

0 - Calm.

1 - Apprehension (because your environment does not feel safe because of the thoughts you are having).

2 - Reassure yourself and remind yourself that you are safe.

3 - Encourage the feeling to pass over you like a wave.

4 - Take slow and deep breaths whilst you remind yourself this moment will pass.

5 - Feel in control.

6 - PRAISE YOURSELF for trying regardless of how far you got.

It takes repetition and consistency
so keep practicing staying calm.

Find your why.
Your motivation, your reason for
wanting to improve your life.
You know this isn't how you want
your life to be, so what motivates
you to keep going?
Perhaps, it's the vision of a better
life, your family, or your unfulfilled
dreams. Whatever it is, write it down
and remind yourself every time your
mind starts to wonder.

# EXPOSURE THERAPY

*Facing your fears until anxiety falls*

Before you throw this book away and shut me down, please hear me out. I get it, I really do. When my Cognitive Behavioural Therapist told me she wanted me to get on the tube and try and venture out four stops, I laughed. I had never heard of exposure therapy before and to be honest, it sounded a little effortless on her part. I waited seven weeks for this session to be told I had to do exactly what I felt, *I couldn't do! If I could get on the train, I would, I explained, but I can't, there's just no way.*

My throat tightened, *I wish I never started therapy, I'm not ready for this, I thought.* Every single sabotaging thought possible entered my mind, I even questioned if I had the right therapist. My barriers were well and truly up! A few days later, I was talking to a friend who had taken her children to London for a day out. My heart sank as mum guilt kicked in. I had endless thoughts of my children not seeing the world, not learning, or exploring unseen places just because of my fears and anxieties. This angered my soul, my children deserved so much more. That day, my anger was amplified; I did something I wished I had done sooner and used my anger as my motivation to get us the hell out.

That week, I got on two trains and visited my dad. *'I don't care if I have a panic attack, I don't care if I pass out anymore. I cannot live like this. I want my life back".* I thought. I was so proud of myself that I emailed my therapist that night. **'Great'**, *she replied. 'But keep doing this, every few days, keep pushing yourself".*

So, with my kids in mind, I did just that. I found my WHY. Not every attempt was a success, some days I just couldn't face the journey but some days I won! I learned to accept that on the days when I didn't go on the journey or didn't fully complete it, at least I tried both mentally and physically. I no longer wanted to be ruled by my fears of what ifs. I wanted more, and I no longer cared about what could happen anymore because the pain of staying trapped inside no longer felt safe, it felt like a wasted life.

## What is Exposure Therapy?

Exposure therapy is an essential component of evidence-based cognitive-behavioural therapy (CBT) treatments for phobia, panic disorder, post-traumatic stress disorder (PTSD), obsessive compulsive disorder (OCD) and social anxiety disorder.

Exposure therapy is exposing yourself to everything your brain is telling you not to. Yes, I know… but you will eventually feel unbelievably powerful. You can do it!

Although exposure therapy sounds difficult it is not impossible. It is useful to think of therapy in the following way.

- Graded (gradually facing your fears)

- Repeated (exposure is repeated)

- Prolonged (stay in an uncomfortable situation for your anxiety to fall by 50% - this can take 30-60 minutes)

**You are only getting short-term relief by escaping and avoiding your fears, but this is not a long-term solution. Exposure therapy will provoke short-term anxiety but lasting relief.**

## Your brains job is to protect you.

When you are faced with something that scares you, but you are NOT actually in real danger, that is your brains way of reminding you of the LAST TIME YOU FELT LIKE THIS.

e.g. I fainted on the train, therefore I avoided the train at all costs because I had convinced myself that I would faint again and be vulnerable. That then spiralled into me not wanting to drive or travel anywhere alone or far from home.

The best way to get through this is to ASK yourself, am I really in danger, or is this just a FEELING because of something that happened in the past?

# PTSD

*Post-traumatic stress disorder is an anxiety disorder caused
by very stressful, frightening, or distressing events.*

These can include:

- Serious road accidents.

- Violent personal assaults, such as sexual assault, mugging or robbery.

- Serious health problems.

- Childbirth experiences.

- Any experience that causes fear, horror, or terror.

## Fact:

Post-Traumatic Stress Disorder can affect anyone.

## Fact:

PTSD can develop immediately after someone experiences a traumatic event, or it can occur weeks, months or even years later.

**People will experience a mental health problem of some kind each year in England.**

## PTSD symptoms

can include anxiety, depression, and flashbacks.

**Suicides were registered in the UK – 2018.**

*Reference: mind.org - The Office for National Statistic –NHS*

# TREATMENTS FOR PTSD

- Talk Therapy.

- CBT – Cognitive Behavioural Therapy.

- EMDR - Eye Movement Desensitisation and Reprocessing.

- Medication.

- Exercise.

- Learning to be present.

- Hypnotherapy.

- Acupuncture.

- Meditation.

- Spending time with people you love.

# PTSD QUESTIONS

*Grab your notebook.*

Are you in a state of panic/fear because of something that happened?
Yes/No

If so, can you identify what that event(s) was?
Yes/No

Do you have physical sensations when thinking about the event?
Yes/No

Do you experience anger or outbursts of anger / frustration, if so, how often?
Yes/No/Sometimes

Do you have difficulty sleeping? This is very common in PTSD sufferers.
Yes/No/Sometimes

Do you experience recurrent nightmares or flashbacks of the event, feeling as though you're in a life-threatening situation again?
Yes/No/Sometimes

Intrusive thoughts are threatening, unexpected thoughts that constantly occur to a person without conscious or voluntary control. These thoughts can create severe anxiety when they enter the mind. They play a vital role in Post-Traumatic Stress Disorder (PTSD), as they have a significant impact on the people affected by it. People with PTSD are stuck in the memories and time during which they experienced the incident and are less attentive to PRESENT in their day-to-day life.

# RATIONALISE THE
# IRRATIONAL THOUGHTS

Trying to rationalise in a moment of anxiety may feel impossible.

So, let's start with small steps.

- Draw out the below diagram in your notebook. Then, write down your anxious thoughts when they come into your mind.

- Try and process your thoughts by categorising them as any of the following.

- The list below helps you soothe, acknowledge, rationalise, and discipline those unhelpful thoughts.

## Thought categories:

- Fact / Non-Fact
- Helpful / Non-Helpful.
- Solution-Focused Outcome.

| Thought | Fact | Not a fact | Helpful | Non Helpful | SF Outcome |
|---|---|---|---|---|---|
| I cannot leave my house. | ❌ | ✅ | ❌ | ✅ | Getting out the house will be good for me. |
| I cannot stop thinking this way | ❌ | ✅ | ❌ | ✅ | I am in control of my thoughts. I am trying to change my thought process. This takes time. |
| I fear I will faint when driving. | ❌ | ✅ | ❌ | ✅ | This has never happened whilst driving. I will take my time. |

No one is coming to save you.
Not everyone will understand you.
Not everyone will care about you.
You have to get up and show up
for yourself, every single day. Life is
too short to live another other way.

# TRAUMA

*"My high functioning anxiety was a result of childhood trauma that lay dormant from the age of 9 until it was triggered when I was 35."*

Trauma is like an invisible anchor around our necks. Just because we cannot see it, doesn't mean it's not there.  Just because a certain number of years have gone past, does not mean that you do not subconsciously hold onto that pain.

A troubled relationship with our parents, a painful break-up, bullying in our adolescence, grief, rejection, disappointment, neglect, abuse, etc… can all affect our belief system which then trickles down to every part of our thinking process in later life.

**People experience trauma at some point in their life.**

**Children and young people**

**are exposed to at least one**

**potentially traumatic event by age 18.**

We cannot just get over certain traumas.
We simply must learn to adapt, adjust, let go and keep living. What happened then is not happening right now. Remind yourself of that every time your mind begins to wonder.

# CHILDHOOD TRAUMA

*Should not be ignored*

I remember being around five or seven years old and going to bed with my panda pouch bag. It had a tiny compartment at the front that I would unzip every night to make sure that in the event of me having to run away, my hairband, tissue, and little beads were safely there to get me through. I'm not sure why I thought I had to run away, I loved my family very much, but something in me was unsettled.

The atmosphere in our home was often tense, my mother battled with Multiple Sclerosis for over ten years. There were always different nurses coming in and out of our home. My father worked three jobs and would often come home stressed and overworked, my brothers and I knew that the best thing we could do was to just stay out of his way. It's hard to be a normal kid when your mother is in the other room, in agony. I often think about my mother's last thoughts, she was only forty years old when she died. Leaving behind four children, ages 22,21,17 and I was 9. Not long after her passing, I was sent to live in North Cyprus with my grandmother. I felt a grief which I had no idea how to process, all I wanted to do was just be with my mother. I didn't want to live without her, I felt a constant pain in my body that I just wanted to stop. I longer wanted to live.

It wasn't until many years later, that I noticed this way of thinking stuck with me. A bad break up with a boyfriend, a loss of a job, basically - any form of abandonment or rejection brought back a massive feeling of loss which overwhelmed me.

**Children that have experienced childhood trauma are;**

**More likely to develop depression**

**More likely to develop anxiety disorders**

My own life experiences inspired me to teach children about the benefits of Mindfulness. Helping children better manage their thoughts, feelings and actions is something I wish was taught in all schools, especially now as many children's lives have been turned upside down by the Covid-19 pandemic.

If you feel your child is suffering from some form of anxiety and it is impacting their day-to-day life, then please speak to a medical professional. I wish my family had.

# TRAUMA QUESTIONS

Please remember, the aim of this book is to dig a little deeper, so work with me. I promise every question has a reason which you will unravel throughout this book. With growth comes discomfort, so if you are feeling a little uncomfortable then we are on the right track.

## How often do you think about a traumatic event(s) that happened to you?

- Daily.
- Every few days.
- Only when something negative happens, making me remember.
- Very rarely. I feel I have processed, grieved and moved on.

## What do you believe about yourself and why?

- You were told something or treated in a way that made you feel less worthy. Therefore, this is impacting your current life.
  Yes/No.

- You experienced disappointment, hurt, and suppressed your feelings, thinking they would just go away. This is impacting your current life.
  Yes/No.

- You are constantly in survival mode making you feel like you can't rely on others for comfort or support. Making you feel emotionally unavailable at times. This way of thinking impacts your current life.
  Yes/No.

## Can you identify how your past is impacting your present moment?

Yes/No

If yes, what could you do to be more present?

If you have mostly answered yes, then you are not alone in feeling this way. The more you realise the true impact of your thoughts impacting your day-to-day life, the more you can learn to reframe the way you think.

I will dive into the power of our thoughts a little further on.

You cannot change past
mistakes or erase your past
memories but you can
choose how you respond
to them now.

# LETTING GO **OF TRAUMA**

*Grab your notebook and a cup of tea*
*(or maybe something stronger... this may take a while)*

**Write down your traumatic event(s) in your notebook or in the back of this book. From birth, until now, what can you remember?**

**How old were you, think about your beliefs / your environment at the time?**

How did you feel, can you remember your thoughts? Write down the date of when the event(s) took place.

Praise yourself, you are simply amazing! Facing the past or something that may be currently upsetting you is not easy. Be immensely proud of yourself for doing this exercise. You could have avoided it, skipped the page, looked the other way but you choose to face it and walk through the memory that is your past, it's not in your present moment and it doesn't have to impact your future anymore.

At the end of the page, write today's date. Look at the date of the event(s) and the present date, how much time has passed between them?

**How is holding onto this memory or belief impacting your current life? Answer the following...**

- Is it stopping you from being happy? Yes/No

- Does it affect your confidence, self-worth, or identity? Yes/No

- What is the most logical solution to help you move forward from this trauma?

- If this trauma wasn't holding you back, how do you think your life would be different? Yes/No – answer fully in your notebook.

Give yourself time to heal.
Getting over a traumatic
experience takes time. Allow
yourself to grieve, give yourself
permission to let go of a
memory that is no longer a
part of your day-to-day life.

# CONTRIBUTING FACTORS TO STRESS & ANXIETY

*Did you know?*

## POOR SLEEP

Sleep problems are very common, research shows that people with chronic insomnia are at high risk of developing an anxiety disorder.

## PAST OR CURRENT TRAUMA

Traumatic events, whether they be from an early incident or one from later in life, can cause anxiety. That is why it is crucial to have healthy coping mechanisms in place to help re-direct your anxious thoughts into a more positive direction.

## POOR GUT HEALTH

A troubled intestine can send signals to your brain, just as a troubled brain can send signals to the gut. Therefore, a person's stomach or intestinal distress can be the cause or the product of anxiety, stress, or depression. That is because the brain and the gastrointestinal system are intimately connected.

## THYROID ISSUES

An overactive thyroid is where the thyroid gland produces too much of the thyroid hormone. This can affect your heart rate and body temperature. Your GP can arrange a blood test for you to check how well your thyroid is working.

## HIGH CORTISOL

As your body perceives stress, your adrenal glands make and release the hormone cortisol into your bloodstream. Often called the stress hormone, cortisol causes an increase in your heart rate and blood pressure. The key is to shift your body from the stress response to the relaxation response.

## EXCESSIVE CAFFEINE

Caffeine does not cause anxiety but too much can make you feel even more wired.

## HORMONE INBALANCES

Women with low progesterone levels and men with low testosterone are prone to anxiety. Estrogen helps stimulate the production and transportation of serotonin around the body and prevents breakdown. Therefore, when oestrogen levels are low, serotonin is also low, and an unstable mood and anxiety can develop.

## THE PILL

Hormonal birth control can cause some side effects such as decreased libido, spotting, and nausea. The mental health side is that it can cause mood swings, depression, and increased feelings of nervousness or anxiety.

## LOW BLOOD SUGARS

Blood sugars drop overnight, leading to low blood sugars in the morning. Low blood sugar can trigger anxiety.

## MINERAL IMBALANCES

Being deficient in certain minerals and vitamins can affect your physical and mental energy.

## INHERITED GRIEF

The newest research in epigenetics tells us that you and I can inherit gene changes from traumas that our parents and grandparents' pain, their fears, their angers, their grief. They can all unwittingly become ours, a legacy we can perpetuate in our family.

You can heal from inherited trauma by allowing yourself to unlearn old habits.

My biggest fear was coming across as mad. I hesitated talking to my doctor, to my family and friends because I feared being judged.
But the truth is, the illusion of having everything figured out. Pretending to be happy when you're not, that is madness.

# HOLISTIC REMEDIES

*Be consistent with adding healthy habits
to your daily routine.*

## SLEEP

Getting enough sleep is vital in improving the functioning of your brain.

- Have a consistent bedtime routine.

- Try and avoid watching movies late into the night, or endlessly scrolling through your phone.

## DRINK MORE WATER

70% of your body is made up of water. This means that dehydration, even as small as 2% can have a negative effect on the brain functions. On average you should drink around 2-3 litres a day.

## DEEP BREATHS

The parasympathetic nervous system is controlled by the vagus nerve, which is the longest cranial nerve in the human body. Deep, diaphragmatic breaths can stimulate the vagus nerve, which sends messages to the brain to relax the body. Blood flow increases, endorphins release, and the sympathetic nervous system is calmed. Breathe...

## EAT WELL

- Avoid processed foods and foods high in sugar.

- Avoid eating late at night.

## REIKI

Reiki is the Japanese name for 'Universal Life Force Energy' which is a life-giving energy present in everyone. It helps promote deep relation and sense of calm.

## CRANIAL THERAPY

Craniosacral therapy us a gentle way to help release symptoms of physical, psychological, and emotional stress.

## ACUPUNTURE

This works by assisting the nervous system to achieve balance. Alleviating stress and anxiety symptoms.

## MEDITATION

Offers you an opportunity to practice focused concentration. Bringing yourself back to the moment and be present. It can help reduce anxiety, depression, heart disease and high blood pressure. Meditation is a habitual process, if you have never meditated before it will take time to adjust, but I promise you will feel the benefits.

## MINDFULNESS

Is being aware of what you are thinking and feeling. Being present in all that you are doing. This especially helps if you yo-yo from the past to the future.

Strength is setting healthy
boundaries.
It's knowing when you need to
stop doing things that make you
miserable.
Stop trying the show the world you
can do it all, your mental health is
the priority, you are the priority.
Nothing else matters.

# FOODS TO HELP BOOST YOUR SEROTONIN

*Serotonin is the key hormone that stabilises our mood, feelings of well-being, and happiness.*

When we get stressed or anxious, our brains release chemicals such as opiates and neuropeptide Y. It's hard to eat well when you're anxious because your brain chemistry is working against your knowledge that you can make better choices.

## Tips:

- Stock up on healthy snacks, prepare healthy meals in advance.
- Batch cook and freeze meals for midweek dinners.
- Avoid buying unhealthy snacks /foods/drinks or keep them out of sight and bring them out for treat/cheat nights only.
- Don't beat yourself up if you do have an extra slice of pizza, it's not worth upsetting yourself over.
- Avoid too much alcohol or smoking.

What amazes me is the amount of dedication we can have towards looking after our external body, our home, our careers, our families, etc. But we spend very little time looking after and protecting our internal mental health and mindset. We take the functioning of our heart, our brain and pretty much all our everyday abilities such as being able to walk, see, hear, feel, smell for granted. But these are the things that help us function and focus, so we must feed our mental health with everything from what we tell ourselves, what we eat, what we drink to what we do.

## Foods to add to your weekly shop.

- Fresh Pineapple
- Eggs
- Cheese
- Tofu
- Salmon
- Nuts & Seeds
- Turkey

- Dark Chocolate
- Blueberries
- Broccoli
- Fatty Fish
- Oranges
- Avocados

## DARK CHOCOLATE & COCOA POWDER

Is a great mood boaster and full of antioxidants.

## PUMPKIN SEED

Contain powerful antioxidants that protect the body and brain from radical damage.

## BROCOLLI

High in vitamin K and packed with antioxidants.

## TURMERIC

Curcumin, the active ingredient in turmeric has shown to cross the blood barrier and directly entering the brain which helps benefit the brain cells. It also works as an anti-inflammatory and is a great antioxidant.

## BLUEBERRIES

Deliver anthocyanins, delivering both anti-inflammatory and antioxidant effects.

## FATTY FISH

60% of your brain is made of fat and half of that is the omega-3.

## ORANGES

Vitamin C is a key factor in preventing mental decline. You can also get a great amount of Vitamin C from strawberries, bell peppers, kiwi and tomatoes.

## AVOCADOS

Are rich in stress-relieving B vitamins and have heart healthy fats that may help lessen anxiety. Vitamin E is a nutrient that is important for vision, reproduction and maintaining healthy skin.

## MAGNESIUM

Is essential for learning & memory. Low magnesium levels are linked to neurological disorders including migraines, depression, and epilepsy.

## IRON

When you have low levels of iron, less oxygen gets to your cells, keeping them from functioning properly and often leading to fatigue, weakness and even anxiety and depression.

## ZINC

This element is crucial for nerve signalling.

## COPPER

Your brain uses Copper to help control your nerve endings.

Are you mindful of
what you put into
your body?

# HAPPY CHEMICALS

## DOPAMINE

**The reward chemical.**

Dopamine helps nerve cells to send messages to each other. It's produced by a group of nerve cells in the middle of the brain and sends out messages to other parts of the brain.

What is the role of dopamine? Dopamine is responsible for allowing you to feel pleasure, satisfaction, and motivation.

**How to naturally produce Dopamine:**

- Completing a task
- Celebrating little wins

## OXYTOCIN

**The love chemical.**

Oxytocin is a hormone and chemical messenger produced in the brain. How to naturally produce Oxytocin:

- Playing with a dog
- Playing with a baby
- Breastfeeding
- Positive physical contact (cuddling, kissing, hugging, holding hands, etc.)
- Social bonding (talking, making eye contact, laughing, etc.)
- Sex/Childbirth

## SEROTONIN

**The happy chemical.**

Serotonin is a neurotransmitter, or chemical messenger, that's involved in many processes throughout your body, from regulating your mood to promoting smooth digestion.

**How to naturally produce Serotonin:**

- Sun exposure.

- Exercise.

- Massage.

- Supplements.
  Pure tryptophan.
  5-HTP.
  SAMe (S-adenosyl-L-methionine).

- Eating probiotic-rich foods, such as yogurt, and fermented foods, such as kimchi or sauerkraut.

**Before trying a new supplement, check in with your healthcare provider. Make sure to tell them if you also take:**

- prescription medication.

- over-the-counter medication.

- vitamins and supplements.

- herbal remedies.

- kimchi or sauerkraut.

# ENDORPHINS

**Endorphins are the body's natural painkillers.**

Endorphins are released by the hypothalamus and pituitary gland in response to pain or stress, this group of peptide hormones both relieves pain and creates a general feeling of well-being.

- Laughing.

- Dark chocolate.

- Exercising.

*Reference: Healthline*

# MIND MAPPING

*Mind mapping lets you structure your thoughts, it allows you to bring order into the chaos of your mind.*

Grab your notebook and sketch out the below mind map. Mind mapping lets you structure your thoughts. No matter how complex an idea or how big a topic, a mind map brings order into the chaos. Make a brief list next to each section. Feel free to add in more categories.

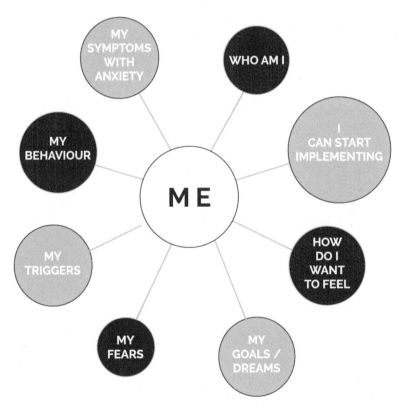

Freedom comes
from challenging your
boundaries of fear.

# LIMITING BELIEFS

*are created by you...*

Limiting beliefs are just thoughts that you have created in your mind. Every time your limiting beliefs tell you that you can't or shouldn't do something, I want you to reject them.

Close your eyes and imagine you have the words STOP – BREATHE - RESET in your mind. As soon as any unhelpful, doubtful thoughts enter your mind, I would like you to focus your attention on slowing down your breathing whilst saying these three words in your mind or out aloud.

If something happened when you were a child or adolescent, then perhaps you did not have the voice or choice to reject or walk away, **but you do right now.**

Bring your mind back to the present moment and know that you are the creator of your belief system so invest the time in creating the best belief system that works for you.

## If you...

- think you are not good enough; you will believe that.

- think you are not capable of securing your ideal job, then you never will.

- think you cannot earn a certain amount of money, then you will be stuck earning a similar amount for the rest of your life.

- think you can never have the ideal weight, then you won't.

- think you are not worthy of love or will never find the right person, then you simply won't.

# BUT HOW CAN I IMPLEMENT CHANGE?

Take baby steps, don't overwhelm yourself with how you will recover. Bite-size your day into digestible chunks and always praise yourself at the end of each day.

When I was at the height of my anxiety, I tried to break my days down to *Morning - Afternoon - Night.*

It's not a great way to live but it made me feel better knowing that now it's lunch time, I've done XYZ, only XYZ left to do then it will be time to do dinner, relaxing bath, read my book and then bed.

Now, I try and be fully present in what I'm doing, I'm productive and enjoying life rather than ticking the days off. But it did not happen overnight, it takes patience, self-love and letting a hell of a lot of S#IT go.

# LIKE A SPLASH OF ICE

Dripping down my back, my anxiety was in full flow, reminding me of everything I could no longer do. I started to become fu#king angry! You're not ruining my children's day again, I thought! I stepped out of the car, trembling with adrenaline, My legs like lead. I made my way into the room of my stepdaughter's birthday party. I refused to sit in the car, I refused to let my anxiety win.

# OBSERVE - PAUSE - RESPOND

Observe your thoughts, pause and decide what is the best way
you can respond.

# STOP

## Doing The Following Today

- Stop procrastinating.

- Stop thinking you are too old or too young.

- Stop chasing someone else's dream.

- Stop comparing your life to others.

- Stop trying to fix other people.

- Stop criticising yourself.

- Stop chasing temporary happiness.

- Stop thinking things will get better on their own.

- Stop ignoring your inner voice.

- Stop feeling guilty for looking after yourself.

- Stop putting others first all the time.

- Stop thinking you have all the time in the world.

- Stop thinking the life you want is not possible for you.

# START

## Doing The Following The Today

- Start believing in yourself.
- Start working towards your dreams.
- Start being fully present in the moment.
- Start accepting your past.
- Start wanting more for your life.
- Start realising you are capable.
- Start talking positively to yourself.
- Start looking after your health.
- Start focusing on your life.
- Start loving yourself again.
- Start showing gratitude for all that you have.
- Start realising that you are enough.

Your happiness and
inner peace are the
goal. You are the goal.

# WORD ASSOCIATIONS

*The words you say to yourself matter.*

The words 'panic attack' as in, something is 'attacking me' is terrifying. Naturally, you will fear the sensations, fuelling more panic to escalate within you.

I read somewhere to use the words 'false alarm' instead and I loved that. Because that's what panic attacks are. It's your lifesaving, fear system kicking in, it thinks you need saving but you DON'T. You are absolutely fine. You are having the sensations because you are constantly in a loop of panic, fear, panic, attack, more fear, OMG am I dying? Etc…The only way to get out of the loop is to **change your relationship** with your false alarm.

I know it's very easy for me to say this whilst I'm sat at my comfy desk drinking a cup of mint tea. However, as someone who has had many false alarms in the past. The most effective way to overcome them is to RIDE OUT THE SENSATION. I get it, I really do. Of course, that sounds ridiculous, it's the total opposite of what your brain is telling you, but I promise you, the more you encourage your body to go through the physical sensations, the quicker you will BREAK THE PATTERN OF PANIC.

It takes time to make big changes to any established routine. So, approach this with BABY STEPS. There will be good days and bad days but eventually the debilitating sensations WILL pass. The panic WILL shrink because you have shown your body and told your brain, that this is nothing to panic about.

# CHANGING YOUR
## INTERNAL DIALOGUE

*For the next 14 days, consciously become AWARE of your internal dialogue. Replace any negative self-talk with the most positive, objective response.*

## Why?

This will help build-on your confidence. Positive self-talk and a more optimistic outlook can have many health benefits. Including increased vitality, greater life satisfaction, improved immune function, reduced pain and better cardiovascular health.

## Avoid Saying Things Like...

- I just can't do that.

- I'm having the day from hell.

- I'm always so ill.

- My life is a nightmare.

- I hate my job.

- I'll never be the weight I want to be.

- I'll never get that job.

- I never have any money.

- Bad things always happen to me.

## Try Saying More Things Like...

- I can do anything I put my energy towards.
- My life is only limited by my beliefs, I deserve more.
- There are other jobs, what works best for me and my commitments?
- I will not compare myself to others. I am doing this for me.
- Today will be whatever I want it to be.
- I attract what I project out to the world.
- I will surround myself with positive people that inspire me.
- I am in charge of my destiny, no one else.

You create your reality. Challenging things happen to everyone. Life is full of wonderful and crazy moments; Focus on the good and learn from the not so good moments.

**So, if our thoughts are so powerful, why are we not showering our minds with endless positive and better serving thoughts."?**

Exactly! If we are not accustomed to this way of thinking, then it will not feel natural. Therefore, your subconscious will resist at first. It will not like the change; it will do everything in its power to revert to your comfort zone. It's crucial to be consistent and replace all negative thoughts with the most positive / neutral outcome you can think of. It will eventually become a new habit.

It can take 21 days to form a new habit. But you have to be consistent and have the desire to want to change.

# I WILL FOCUS ON WHAT I CAN CONTROL

## Things that are in my control

My words

My actions

How I treat others

How I respond

How I take care of myself

My decisions

## Things that are out of my control

What other people do or say

Things from the past

Other people's choices

How other people feel

# WHAT IF...

*What if you created the life you truly wanted?*

Start replacing your negative "what ifs "with positive, **factual** what ifs.

Has that scary thought happened, what are the chances of it happening, or is it just a thought based on something that happened in the past? If so, we need to tell your brain to get over it. It's happened, I'm safe. Now let me live my life!

## Replacing your what ifs...

| | | |
|---|---|---|
| What if I get in the car and crash? | *or* | What if I take my time, drive 5mins a day to help my recovery? |
| What if I get on the train and faint? | *or* | What if I take a friend at first and try? I can always leave if I want to. |
| What If I have another panic attack? | *or* | What if I try and focus on the activity rather than my thoughts? |
| What if I feel trapped in the shops? | *or* | What if I don't, I can always leave if it gets busy. |
| What if something awful happens? | *or* | What if I have a great day? |
| What if I lose control? | *or* | What if I remind myself that I am in control? |
| What if I fail? | *or* | What if I'm a success? |
| What if I regret this decision? | *or* | What if it ends up being the best decision you've ever made? |

# WHAT IF YOU DID THIS EXERCISE

Write down your what ifs and try and replace them with positive what ifs. I know it may seem unrealistic at the moment but what we are trying to do is stimulate your brains neuropaths to change its patterns of thinking. We are trying to feed it with a new perspective.

| | | |
|---|---|---|
| What if | *or* | What if |
| What if | *or* | What if |
| What If | *or* | What If |
| What if | *or* | What if |
| What if | *or* | What if |
| What if | *or* | What if |
| What if | *or* | What if |
| What if | *or* | What if |

Believe you can change,
Believe in yourself enough to
take daily action.
Soon, you will see the results,
I promise you that.

# STOP CATASTROPHSING...

Imagining and believing that the worst possible thing will happen.

It's quite an unrealistic place to be, and very unhelpful. Always believing the worst is disempowering too.

What's most likely to happen? If the worst does happen, can you cope and accept the consequences?

# MINDSET RESET

*Mindset is everything*

You attract what you project out to the world.

Just because you have lived in a certain state of habitual thinking for a long period of time, doesn't mean you cannot change your mindset. The reason many people find it so hard to change is because they do not believe they can. Becoming consciously aware of any unhealthy habits or thinking patterns and changing them daily, is exhausting. Change is excruciatingly hard in the beginning; it takes a hell of a lot of self-discipline, self-love and consistency but it can be done. The first step is, changing your attitude.

Step 1: Believe you can change.

Step 2: Learn to change your attitude.

Step 3: Allow yourself to grow.

Step 4: Make small lifestyle changes and stick to them.

When we begin to understand how our mindset is formed, it allows us to have a much easier time resetting our current beliefs. Some of the earliest influences in shaping our thoughts come from.

- The people who cared for us.
- Who we associated with, friends and our relationships.
- Who influenced us.
- Labelled us.
- Watch we see / hear on TV/ Radio / social media.

**Fact:** People will NOT change until they make a conscious decision to change.

**Fact:** 95% of all our behaviours & reactions happen at a subconscious level. The majority of what we do daily is done in AUTOPILOT.

**Fact:** The reason many people give up or find it too difficult to change old habits because our conscious thinking requires a higher thinking power which can feel exhausting in the beginning.

**Fact:** Thoughts are not facts; they are made up of ideas that we create in our minds. Thoughts associated with a horrible feeling, lead to a negative reaction. That's why it is so crucial to try and associate a thought with a positive feeling.

# HOW COULD YOU START YOUR DAY WITH THE RIGHT MINDSET?

Starting your day with the right mindset is key. Your attitude, beliefs and thoughts all contribute to the kind of day you will experience. A positive mindset takes time, especially if you are used to thinking a certain way so give yourself time and be consistent.

When you wake up in the morning, what are your first thoughts? Are they positive or negative? If you are thinking about your endless to-do list, debt, heartache, or stresses, then you will only attract more of those things into your life.

## NOURISH YOUR MIND

With the most positive version of yourself in mind. Think of the woman or man you want to become; be the person you would look up to. How would they do things differently?

## START TO DO THINGS DIFFERENTLY

- If you usually roll over and check your phone, then do things differently today. Start your morning with gratitude for another day. Positive affirmations, breathing exercises, a healthy routine and most of all, a plan for yourself.

- Set realistic and achievable intentions. If you set yourself unrealistic intentions for the day, you will only feel worse if you do not complete them.

- Write your intentions down and tick them off during the day.

If we want to reprogram and change any habits or unhelpful ways of thinking, we need to become consciously aware of them. The conscious part of the brain streams electrical impulses which are indirectly related to what is going on in your world. What you can see, smell, feel, hear. It involves our HIGHER thinking capacity.

## SUBCONSCIOUS MIND

- Learned behaviours & habits.
- Fight & flight response.
- Records & stores all of our experiences & knowledge, forming memories.
- Emotional mind
- Cannot determine the difference between that which is real or what is imagined.
- Must always accept info from your conscious mind.

## CONSCIOUS MIND

- Info from the TV / Internet / Other people / your environment.
- You can choose to accept or reject information.
- Your conscious mind is your objective or thinking mind.
- It has no memory, and it can only hold one thought at a time.
- What we see, feel, smell and hear comes from our conscious mind.

Sometimes, when everything feels too much. I close my eyes and take myself to my happy place. Nothing else matters here. I'm simply relaxing under the beaming sun, on a private yacht, shades on, sipping a mojito. Absolute bliss.

Where is your happy place?

Ps: I've never been on a yacht, let alone a private yacht. But I can dream…

# HOW TO BREAK A HABIT

*Loop of thoughts*

Be consistent with your new routine, if you're constantly yo-yo from unhealthy habits to good then it will feel impossible to build up momentum. You have to find the power within you to keep going. Remember to find your WHY, why is it important for you to break away from your non-serving habits?

## Think of your brain as a circuit.

- One wire splitting into two wires.

- At the end of each wire is a possible outcome.

- One positive, one negative.

- But since our brain's job is to keep us safe, the "wire" leading to the worst outcome is a lot thicker.

- Our brain impulse travels down that wire to the worst outcome.

Therefore, taking the time to create the best possible outcome and allowing new circuits to form, is vital. What you feed your mind is based on your thoughts being a little stuck, so if we want to create better thoughts we must think and try to believe them. (I know, it's not easy) But we need to train our brain to create a new thick 'positive' wire.

## How do I know when my new habit(s) have taken effect?

When it becomes instinctive.

When you learned to read and write, you did not learn these abilities by just sitting down for one day and acquiring them. It took practice, patience, and repetition.

What we want to do is go from habitual behaviour (**subconscious behaviour**) to self-awareness (**conscious behaviour**) to then instinctive positive behaviour.

## What is it YOU really want and what is stopping you from getting it?

It's the small daily changes.
How you choose to spend your
mornings, how you internally
talk to yourself, what you absorb
from the outside world. What you
read, watch, and who you spend
your time with... It's the small
healthy habits that can make a big
difference to your day-to day life.

# PROCRASTINATION

*Is a habit*

You've had a long list of things you need to do but somehow you have found every possible excuse… sorry I mean 'valid reason' to just not do them. If so, then you are a true procrastinator.

Do you hear yourself saying things like, I'm too tired, I'll do it tomorrow…I'll just do it when the weather is better? I'll do it when I have more time. But if you are truly honest with yourself, you are probably avoiding that mundane task because you really don't want to do it.

Kickstarting momentum isn't easy, especially if your brain is so used to putting things off.

**of us are affected to some degree by procrastination.**

**of us procrastinates every single day.**

# HOW TO STOP PROCRASTINATING

## GET ORGANISED

Write down what needs to be done in your day.

Do this in priority order and be realistic with what you can manage with your current commitments.

## BITE-SIZE YOUR DAY

Bite-size your day into chunks. Split your day into, AM – NOON – PM. Listing what needs to be done and ticking your list as you go along.

## SET A TIME

Set yourself a 10–15-minute timer to get started on whatever it is you're avoiding. Once started, stop at 10-15mins, and keep doing this every day and increasing the timer by 5-20mins. Once you build up momentum, you will do it. It's just finding ways to start.

## TAKE RESPONSIBILITY

Accept responsibility and accountability for the things you do NOT do.

## PARENT YOURSELF

Remember when you were a kid, and your parents would be on at you to make your bed and to put your shoes away? Sometimes, we have to do the same for ourselves because let's be honest, there are many things I really don't want to do as an adult. Cooking every bloody day is one of them but I do it because apparently, I'm a responsible adult with children.

## REMINDERS

Leave yourself reminders on your phone of why you should get XYZ done and just do it!

## SELF-PRAISE

Praise yourself once you have completed your task. How do you feel? Reward yourself.

## KEEP BUILDING MOMENTUM

Keep going even when that little annoying voice tells you not to.

Remind yourself that your subconscious mind does not like change, it will do all that it can to revert you back to your comfort zone, so you must learn to acknowledge those sabotaging thoughts but don't feed them. You simply carry on with what you want to get done.

Keep focused and continue creating the best version of your life.

Just start!

# STOP – BREATHE – PLAN

*How to get what you want*

What does a successful life look like to you? Think about what it is you truly want and write it down. Go back to your mind map or create a new one. When you know what you want, regardless of all your sabotaging thoughts… Make a plan and stick to it.

## Tips:

- It can be a daily, weekly, or monthly plan but start small and don't overwhelm yourself in the beginning.

- Be consistent and keep the momentum going.

- I have a daily to-do list and a journal, once I'm up and showered I write my to-dos for the day. It helps me navigate in a much more productive way.

- Take the time to learn and explore new ideas.

- Be prepared to make mistakes and learn from them. Don't be ruled by your ego.

- Visualise what it is you truly want, do this every morning and before bed.

- Be disciplined and believe in your dreams and desire enough to create them.

- Listen to your intuition. The universe will work with you if you allow yourself to let go of all the noise in your mind. This is why meditation is so powerful. Once you learn to quieten the inner noise, your intuition will be so high that your vibration will completely shift towards manifestation.

- Do not let other people's opinions discourage you. Most importantly, START.

# STOP – BREATHE – CREATE

- If you want to become a writer, then start writing.
- If you want to become a singer, then sing.
- If you want to learn how to start your own business, research, learn, explore ideas, and don't be afraid to fail.
- If you want to go back to studying, book a course. Stop hesitating.
- If you want to live abroad, do it.
- If you want more time for yourself create it.

Stop waiting for that big moment when everything will fall into place and then you'll do all the things you really wanted to do.

Stop blaming your current circumstances for all the things you are not doing. If you really want to do something, take the time and just do it.

## "BUT it's not that easy"

It's excruciatingly hard to get past the self-sabotaging thoughts, the limiting beliefs, and sometimes even major financial sacrifice. But do you honestly want to spend your life playing it safe, one day, wishing you had taken more chances and just allowed yourself to truly be happy? You deserve that.

## What do you want for your life and why?

Write it down today, be as honest as possible.

# STOP – BREATHE – BELIEVE

*Create your Bucket List*

It's important to set goals for yourself, and a bucket list does just that. Bucket lists give you purpose, focus, and a healthy direction for your life.

Grab your notebook and create your bucket list. Do not listen to any sabotaging thoughts, just write down everything you desire.

What do you want to see, explore, learn, achieve, and create?

What do you want to add to your life experiences?

Set goals for yourself, get out there and discover something new. Make the most of the one life you have.

List 5 -10 things you would like to add to your bucket list. If you can't think of 10 then please just add as you go along, you do not have to add everything today. Start with just a few and set yourself a plan to make these dreams happen.

## Tips:

- Look at your bucket list daily and add or tick off as you go along.

- Set a realistic time frame for when you would like to achieve your goal(s). Putting a date next to your goals helps give you a sense of focus.

- Create a mood board. It helps keep your mind constantly aware of accomplishing your life goals. Even when you're not looking directly at your board, your subconscious mind will be tuned in to its presence.

- Commit to your dreams and goals.

- Do not give up just because something did not materialise when you expected it to. Keep believing in yourself and keep going.

# 10

# REASONS WHY CHANGE FEELS HARD

1 We get stuck in a pattern of looping behaviour.

2 We think we are not capable of changing or worthy of the life we desire.

3 We simply do not feel we have the energy to get ourselves out of the mental hole.

4 We think we are too young, too old, too fat, too skinny, too tired, too different, not educated enough, not popular enough, not wealthy enough or not beautiful enough. Essentially, we think we are simply not enough.

5 We do not dedicate consistent time for growth.

6 We lose confidence in our abilities and strengths.

7 We think this is just who we are and who we will always be.

8 We feel controlled by our thoughts.

9 We do not feel supported.

10 We do not see a way out.

Be patient and kind to yourself.
Good things are coming your way.
Everything is going to be ok.
Things have a way of working out.
Life is so short; todays worries will
seem small in a years' time.
Keep going.

# HAVING THE RIGHT ATTITUDE ABOUT MONEY

Many of my clients have struggled with believing that they deserve more financial freedom.

If you come from a lack of financial freedom, you may THINK you CANNOT achieve a certain salary. However, this is completely untrue, most wealthy people come from a financially challenging background. The only difference they had between success and poverty was the DETERMINATION to not give up on their dreams and goals.

I'm a huge believer in the Law of Attraction and a big fan of Bob Proctor, Marisa Peer, and Mel Robbins. You may have heard of Bob Proctor from The Secret, if you haven't then I suggest looking him/them up. I study their material often and they have endless videos and invaluable resources on their websites.

## Tips:

- Know your worth, do not undervalue yourself in business.
- Carry money on you so you can visually see money in your purse or wallet.
- When you pay for something, regardless of how big or small, show thanks rather than guilt.
- Learn to help others if you can, it does not have to be big amounts. By giving back, you are creating a positive energy for yourself and others.
- Think of how you could make money from multiple sources.

- Reject negative money thoughts.

- Surround yourself with people that inspire you.

- BELIEVE that you can create the income you desire

- Stop saying things like - I can never afford that. I'll never earn that kind of money, that life is not for the likes of me.  Become mindful of how you talk to yourself about money and start making a conscious effort to replace any negative self-talk or negativity with the most positive thing you could say to yourself.

## PLEASE DO NOT

Focus on debt and bills.  Focus your attention on how you can objectively find solutions rather than consume your mind with worry and fear. As a single mother with two children, I know this is not easy and how hard this can be. But when you train your mind to look at the solutions, rather than the negative aspects, ideas flow, your energy changes and just like magic, things start to shift.

# STOP – BREATHE – ORGANISE

*Organising your day = organising your life*
*= organising your mind.*

If everything around you feels chaotic then your mind will represent that. Keep your home and your workspace clear of clutter and mess. Think of your home as a representation of your mind, how would you like your mind to look?

Create a space that makes you feel calm and relaxed. Somewhere you can feel positive and inspired, not stressed or overwhelmed. Remove things you no longer use or need, store them out of sight or if you feel ready, give them away.

## START YOUR DAY WITH POSITIVE INTENTION

Be honest, what is your morning routine like? I remember a time when my mornings were the most stressful part of my day. Trying to get both kids up and out, whilst getting myself ready for work and out of the house at 7.30am was beyond stressful. I would be eating a slice of toast whilst screaming at the kids to put their shoes on for the millionth time. I was not setting my day with any positive intentions.

## WHAT WOULD MAKE YOU FEEL GOOD TODAY?

Not just externally, but internally? I know for me getting the millionth wash load done is weirdly satisfying but it doesn't feed my soul. It's just a completed task. Reading a few pages of my book, having a coffee with a friend, helps me switch off from my usual day-to-day life. What feeds your soul?

# WALKING AWAY

*from what doesn't feel right*

It took me nearly twelve years to find the strength to walk away from a relationship that wasn't right. I ignored my gut feeling and many red flags because I hoped that things would change. I didn't want a failed marriage, I didn't want my children to come from a broken home, I was so absorbed by what I didn't want that I completely lost focus on what I did want or need.

I would often think and hope that things will change. *When we came back from our family vacation, things will be better. When we move home, he'll be happier. When the kids are at school, there will be less pressure. When he gets that promotion, he'll be more relaxed.*

Things never changed, they got worse.

When faced with external pressures of family expectations, children, and financial commitments, it's enough to make you stay in the hope that things will improve… one day.

But how long can you hold onto hope, when is the cut-off point?

Having a healthy mindset and self-confidence is key in helping you make better choices in any relationship. Low self-esteem can cause you to sabotage good relationships or settle for ones where you're treated badly.

No relationship is perfect. However, if something hasn't felt right for a long time, if your sense of identity is being compromised then you need to start asking yourself some uncomfortable questions.

- Do you believe things will change with time? If so, how long have you waited already? Has much changed?

- Is this the relationship you imagined?

- Does your partner bring out the best in you?

- Do you make endless excuses for your partner?

- Do they stand by you in hard times or have you and your children in mind when living out their life?

Compromise, flexibility, and adjustments are always a part of a healthy relationship. But, if your partner does not show you the same respect you endlessly keep on showing them, something needs to change.

**Anxiety in a relationship can make you overly dependent or avoidant:**

### If you are dependant

- Constantly seeking support and reassurance.
- Fear rejection.
- Over-thinking.
- Constantly want to please.

### If you are avoidant

- Maybe thought of as cold.
- Emotionally unavailable.
- Lacking empathy / stand-offish.
- Avoid intimacy.

If you are lucky enough to be with someone who understands when you feel overwhelmed, or when you don't enjoy certain situations or places, then that's great.

But if you don't, then that will just add more anxiety and pressure. Not everyone will understand why you do or say the things you do, but that doesn't mean they don't care.

Anxiety has a way of stopping you from enjoying so much, and at times can make you feel so isolated from the rest of the world. It's important to be honest about how you feel, just because you feel this way now does not mean you always will.

## Tips:

- Be honest about what you need from your partner, what would help you in moments of overwhelm?
- Don't struggle in silence. Reach out to friends/talk to your partner.
- Set boundaries. It's important to have boundaries in life. Determine what your priorities are and what you will accept from others in life.
- Learn to trust yourself and not to always depend on your partner.
- Spend quality time with your partner and communicate in a healthy way.
- Don't try and control everything. Learn to let go a little.
- Avoid making everything a problem. Anxiety heightens everything.
- Don't try and change someone. People only change if they want.
- Don't make excuses for someone's bad behaviour. Someone's traumatic past doesn't mean they can destroy your present moment or your future.
- Learn to love and trust yourself.

In an attempt to fix him.
I broke myself beyond
recognition.

# TOXIC PEOPLE

Speak badly about others.

Are negative.

Take up way too much of your time.

Constantly have drama going on.

Lie to you.

Criticize you.

Play the victim.

Have to be right.

Are self-obsessed.

Have addiction issues.

Treat others poorly.

Try to control.

Lack compassion.

Constantly have drama going on.

## Sue Fitzmaurice

You can have all the
knowledge in the
world, but if you don't
put it into action and
practice what you
know. It's wasted.

# SOUL vs EGO

Feed your soul. The soul focuses on what makes you feel content, grateful, happy, fulfilled, excited, etc.

The ego focuses on what makes you feel powerful, superior, and important. It's an identity we construct from our beliefs. If we learn to combine both SOUL & EGO, then we can master amazing things. Ego on its own is destructive and artificial.

# PEOPLE PLEASING

Is a deep-rooted fear normally from childhood. Fear of rejection, failure or basing happiness on external validation.

In life we will fail. We will be judged by others; we will let family or friends down at times and… that's OK.

Don't be afraid of losing people.
Be afraid of losing yourself
at the expense of pleasing others.

You are not a measure
of your professional education,
your job, or the certificates
hanging up on the wall.
You are what you believe
yourself to be, so start believing
in yourself.

Your subconscious mind cannot determine what is real and what isn't. Imagine what you want is already yours, create who you want to become. You will attract whatever you put out to the universe.

# GRATITUDE BREATHWORK

*Helps calm down the nervous system*

Daily breathwork allows you to bring your anxious nervous system back to a state of peace, calm and clarity. Breathing exercises can help activate the parasympathetic, which controls your rest state, and deactivate the sympathetic nervous system which regulates your fight-or-flight response, with stimulation of the vagus nerve.

I was always quite dismissive of breathwork exercises and techniques, the thought of taking the time to just sit and breathe felt a little pointless. However, it wasn't until I pushed through the self-sabotage that I noticed a huge difference emotionally and physically.

**Find a quiet and peaceful place in your home to take 5-10 minutes a day to quieten your mind and focus on what is going right in your life.**

- Lay down
- Place your hands on your stomach

Inhale - in from your nose, 1,2,3,4 (hold your breath for 1 second)
*Breathe in peace, clarity, love, abundance (whatever you want to feel)*
Exhale – from your mouth 1,2,3,4
*Breathe out, anxiety, worries, anger, tension, (whatever you want to let go)*

Think about....

- What is great in my life?
- What is working in my life?
- I am grateful for.
- I am open to receiving love and abundance.
- I focus on what is going right in my life

# NAKED MIRROR EXERCISE

*Helps with Confidence*

Be honest, are you comfortable looking at yourself?

For most people, loving themselves does not come naturally. Loving others, showering others with endless praise and love, however, just rolls of our tongues but when we receive it back it's just uncomfortable. Cringy in fact.

If you can relate then this page is for you, the first step to building on your confidence is learning to believe in yourself, your abilities and your strengths. It's learning to embrace and love all of you, even the parts that are hidden away.

For us to become comfortable with the parts of us we do not like, we have to become uncomfortable. So get naked or keep your underwear on, it's totally up to you.

### To do

- Take 5-10 minutes to stand or sit in front of a mirror.
- Look at yourself.
- Breathe in and out deeply.
- Notice your body moving.
- Become aware of any unhelpful thoughts.

## Think about

- What kind words could you say when those unhelpful, habitual thoughts show up?

- Do you accept all of you? If not, why?

- What parts of you do you like/dislike?

- Your journey up until now, what has your body carried you through?

- Love yourself like you love others, why? Because you deserve that.

- Remind yourself that you are enough. Just the way you are.

- Repeat the affirmations on the next page.

## Tips:

- Delete any social media accounts that make you feel like shit.

- Don't compare yourself to others.

- Allow yourself to grow and change.

- Stop punishing / shaming yourself.

- Never give up on you

# Affirmations:

Whilst looking in the mirror, try and connect a feeling with the words you are saying, feel the words and most importantly, believe in them. Feeling connects power to the words so at first, you might not believe in them but keep doing this every morning and soon you will feel the energy take over you.

- I love you (say your name).
- I love all that you do for me.
- I am grateful for my life.
- I am good enough.
- I love my smile, my shoulders, my stomach, my legs, my toes.
- I am confident I will have the life I want.
- I am capable, I am strong.
- I deserve to be happy.
- I am unique and that is my power,
- There is no such thing as perfect.
- I am deserving of love

Anything you can imagine,
you can create.

*-Oprah Winfrey.*

# VISUALISATION EXERCISE

*If you can see it, you can be it.*

Allow your imagination to think big. Visualisation exercises will enable you to train and stimulate your unconscious mind to operate out of a new perspective more easily.

To do

1. Sit upright with your back straight but comfortable.
2. Close your eyes (after reading this) and focus on your breathing.
3. Take deep, slow breaths in from your nose and exhale from your mouth. Do this 3 - 4 times.

Roll your shoulders back and then forth to allow any knots in your shoulders to unwind. Allow the warm and relaxing feeling to penetrate your muscles and bones. Feeling the tingling in your toes as your inner energy moves around your body.

4. Be specific with your imagination, what is it you want; (here are just a few examples)

Inner peace • Better health • Fulfilment • Confidence • Financial freedom • New Career / Home / Car • Love.

5. Take a moment to connect with what it is you really want.

6. I want you to picture seeing yourself, in a place which makes you feel calm and relaxed. It could be anywhere. Try not to overthink, just allow your mind to guide you a little.

7. This version of yourself is your most relaxed, happiest, and most confident.

**What is she/he doing right now? - How does this version of yourself talk, walk, behave, think?**

**What can you hear, smell, see, feel in your heart? - How does this new perspective make you feel?**

**If you could take away one thing from this version if yourself, what would it be?**

Do this for 5-10 minutes a day for 14 days and you will start to notice the difference.

Allow your intuition to guide you and create the life you want. The more you visualise, the more you will get better at it. It does take time. If you think you cannot get out of your current situation, visualise everything you want as if it's ALREADY HAPPENING. How does that make you feel?

Everything always
works out in the end.
Sometimes even better
than you could have
ever imagined.
Trust your intuition and
don't be afraid to walk
away from the things
that don't  bring you joy.

# NOTE TO READER

*Thank you for allowing me to be apart of your journey.*

We are at the end of this book but perhaps we're at the very beginning or in the midst of your self-discovery journey. Growth is a never-ending journey of allowing yourself to live a truly authentic life. Regardless of your background, circumstances, or lifestyle choices, you deserve to be happy, you deserve to have the life you dream about because nothing is out of your reach.

At times I have questioned my sanity, my purpose, my very own identity, the more I tried to find out why I felt the way I did, the more confused and isolated I felt. Put your attention on how you want to feel, learn something new, call an old friend that you know will be good for your soul. You are in control of the next chapter of your life, only you can decide where you are going from here. Make a choice.

Amongst the chaos, there is always beauty.

Sending love always. x

# TALK

*You are not alone.*

It's time for anyone who has or is suffering with their mental health to speak up. Reach out and communicate to the friend you haven't heard from in a while. Perhaps there's a friend that recently lost their job, a single parent who is struggling to get by or simply just your neighbour whom you haven't seen for a while. Support & love yourself and others. For me knowing that others felt the same way as I did, made me feel less alone, less mad.

Please seek professional support if you are feeling overwhelmed. You do not have to suffer, and it could change your life for the better. Apart from talking to your GP or a therapist, here are a few supportive websites based in the UK.

Anxietyuk.org.uk

Mind.org.uk

Nopanic.org.uk

Telephone helplines UK

**The Samaritans** – 116 123 (available 24/7)

**Saneline** – 0300 304 7000 (available daily 16.30 – 22.30)

Printed in Great Britain
by Amazon

80789270R00099